Bobby G. Bell
Wingate College
10

D0810622

EMOTIONAL COMMON SENSE

EMOTIONAL

COMMON SENSE

HOW TO AVOID
SELF-DESTRUCTIVENESS

ROLLAND S. PARKER

1817

HARPER & ROW, PUBLISHERS

New York, Evanston, San Francisco, London

Wingate College Library

EMOTIONAL COMMON SENSE: HOW TO AVOID SELF-DESTRUCTIVENESS. Copyright © 1973 by Rolland S. Parker. All rights reserved. Printed in the United States of America. No part of this book may be used or reproduced in any manner whatsoever without written permission except in the case of brief quotations embodied in critical articles and reviews. For information address Harper & Row, Publishers, Inc., 10 East 53rd Street, New York, N.Y. 10022. Published simultaneously in Canada by Fitzhenry & Whiteside Limited, Toronto.

Designed by Sidney Feinberg

Library of Congress Cataloging in Publication Data

Parker Rolland S
  Emotional common sense.

  Bibliography: p.
  1. Conduct of Life. 2. Emotions. I. Title.
BF637.C5P35   158'.1   72-9758
ISBN 0-06-013278-7

---

*This book is dedicated to Professor Zygmunt A. Piotrowski,
my friend and doctoral adviser, in appreciation for his efforts
on my behalf when I was a student, and later.*

Contents

Foreword

In contrast to most psychotherapeutic approaches which are necessarily restricted to the few because of a limitation in available personnel as well as the cost of services, Dr. Parker's "do it yourself" approach in *Emotional Common Sense* offers hope to the many. Consequently, it is entirely appropriate that his chapter concerning advice on choosing a psychotherapist is placed at the end of the book.

The book is designed to help the reader utilize his own resources effectively in order to lead a happier and more productive life. It is earthy, practical, occasionally humorous, and completely without the special jargon which is a feature of so many recently published works in the field of psychotherapy. Soundly based on modern behavioral science, it also synthesizes the shared experiences of many individuals who have spoken about their problems and the solutions they utilize in Dr. Parker's weekly Participation/Discussion groups.

The author has practiced group and individual psychotherapy, psychodiagnosis, research, executive career counseling, and management consultation. The book illustrates the many ways in which people are self-destructive, e.g., make damaging decisions because they lack self-awareness; have unfounded ideas about social relationships and their own personality; follow false values, and seek momentary gratifications without regard for the consequences. *Emotional Common Sense* is a practical approach to increasing understanding of oneself and improving social relationships, with the goal of improving one's life style, recognizing and avoiding stress, and achieving meaningful goals.

It is demonstrated that people ought not to trust their feelings automatically because of the defective way in which the human brain places reliance upon experiences carried over from childhood. Included are self-evaluation sections and special tools for understanding your values, needs, life style, social relationships, emotional discomforts, and frustrations of employment. Special chapters discuss the basis for and techniques of coping with stress, guilt, anxiety, feelings of worthlessness, loneliness, dependency, interpersonal antagonism, irrational anger, depression, inability to be self-assertive, and sexual self-destructiveness. The approach is designed to help in relationships with mates, children, employees, and anyone with whom one comes into meaningful, close contact. Finally, practical advice is offered for choosing a psychotherapist, if this is required to break the cycle of self-destructiveness.

The author's unique and valuable service has been to make available in practical, usable form many of the central tenets of psychological theory and practice while at the same time recognizing the complexity of many of the issues at hand. His contention, for example, that the ability to experience anger is present at birth will be disputed by many, but Dr. Parker takes note of this and, at the same time, makes a cogent case for his point. Another assumption, namely, that neither pain nor anger dissipate over time but will have inevitable, negative repercussions unless properly dealt with is grounded in the classical psychoanalytic theory of development and is one that is not shared by all thinkers in the field. Dr. Parker bravely opens the Pandora's box of woman's changing role in current society and in this male's opinion gives appropriate credence to the effects of biology, historical and social conditions, and economics. He deals with the here and now and has not carried this idea to Margaret Mead's vision of a future in which "parenthood would be limited to a smaller number of families whose principal functions would be child rearing" and the implications which this would have for the development of woman's social role.

As a practicing psychiatrist who also teaches, supervises, and works on a team with fellow professionals in clinical psychology and social work, I am in general agreement with Dr. Parker's approach to training, criteria for therapist selection, and treatment approaches. I see us as allies in the same basic tasks and, indeed, the team approach which is widely used at present has frequently led to interchange of functions between psychiatrists, psychologists, social workers and other team members. However, a role that is specific to the psychiatrist is the prescribing of psychotropic medications whose value in the relief of certain target symptoms (in anxiety, depression) has been established. By the same token complex psychological testing and research protocols must be assigned to the appropriate professionals. Also, while recognizing Dr. Parker's point that psychiatric training can be improved, it is important to note that the training of the modern psychiatric resident has vastly changed from its previous intrainstitutional orientation, for the current emphasis is on work with ambulatory patients. In the institutions with which I am affiliated the residents spend more than two-thirds of their time with ambulatory patients and, in addition, about 80 percent of these residents are in concurrent personal or didactic analysis.

What has *Emotional Common Sense* to offer to distinguish it from many works of its genre? It is a book that is firmly rooted in humanistic values, soundly based in psychological principles and amply infused with the basic common sense of an experienced, skilled practitioner. Consistent with the author's practical and realistic approach is his recognition that in some cases the intervention of a psychotherapist is needed.

—JAMES I. HANNON, M.D.

New York City
February 1973

Preface

This book is written to enable the reader to improve his emotional well-being, social relationships, and decision-making abilities through increased understanding both of himself and others. The contrasting concepts of emotional common sense and self-destructiveness are set forth as tools for recognizing and then eliminating the hazards caused by the games, exploitations, and irrational angers of others. Emotional common sense implies that the reader, were he a dispassionate bystander, could advise himself as the actor on far superior ways of relating to others in order to improve his frame of mind and productiveness. Self-destructiveness means acting against one's best interests, particularly when the harmful consequences can be readily predicted. Through understanding his needs, drives, values, and life style, the reader is encouraged to develop ways of relating that lead to greater warmth in the exchange with others and, at the same time, to recognize and avoid people who endanger self-respect and who create emotional discomfort.

I decided that I would tell it the way it is, that I would be truthful to the point of bluntness about the way people behave: basely, ludicrously, and without self-respect. By understanding the content of this book and following some of the practical guidelines toward self- and social understanding, the reader can improve his emotional life. To obtain this objective, a variety of suggestions that have proven successful on how to improve social relations have been included.

My point of view evolved from my observations of people as a personal participant, psychotherapist, and leader of public Participation/Discussion groups around meaningful emotional topics. About three thousand individuals have expressed their feelings, shared their concerns, and offered personal solutions which they found helpful in coping with emotional distress. All of this observation and collective wisdom I have tried to synthesize in a professionally sound way. My approach is eclectic; it avoids the limitations of any particular school of psychological thought.

To help the reader clarify his needs, values, and attitudes and to learn why he experiences emotional discomfort, I have described the development of many key areas of personality. I have also included some self-help questionnaires and check lists which are derived from the emotional problems experienced by many people in daily living with mates, children, friends, employment, etc.

I would particularly like to express my thanks to Jane Morrin, who provided invaluable aid in the functioning of the G.R.O.W. Participation/Discussion series, my patients, and the participants in the public meetings who provided so much richness of human experience included here.

I am very grateful to Harold Grove for the many hours of editorial work he devoted to the manuscript in its preparation for publication. As a result of his labor, the text has been improved in a number of significant ways.

R.S.P.

New York City
November 1972

Art is long, life short, judgment difficult, opportunity transient. To act is easy, to think is hard; to act according to our thought is troublesome. Every beginning is cheerful: the threshold is the place of expectation.

    —GOETHE, *Wilhelm Meister's Apprenticeship,*
      Translated by Thomas Carlyle

EMOTIONAL COMMON SENSE

1   *Self-Destructiveness*

Most people are self-destructive. They behave in ways that are obviously against their best interest. They hurt themselves even though they know better. You the reader are probably self-destructive. Can you really assert that there is nothing that you have done yesterday or today that is not in your best interest? Would it be a safe bet that you just obtained a momentary satisfaction from an action which is against your preferred style of life or goals or values? Perhaps you have antagonized somebody important or neglected to build up an important relationship.

Self-destructiveness does not always result in suicide, although that is frequently the end result. Self-destructiveness means creating circumstances that ruin relationships, reduce creativity, permit others to take advantage, or continue harmful contacts with others in the name of "family" or "friendship" or "security." Self-destructiveness means not listening to others' needs and messages, thus enduring conflict and disappointment. Self-destructiveness means seeing oneself as valueless, becoming the target of someone's irrational anger, the patsy of the exploitative grasper, or the self-selected wallflower of life.

Self-destructiveness is also remaining unaware of one's own needs for support, for love, for self-assertion. It is laziness that

1

demands immediate satisfaction as opposed to the long-range discipline of accomplishment. Paradoxically, self-destructiveness is also the excessive sacrifice of time, money, and love for unattainable long-range goals so that years go by which are wasteful of enjoyment and vitality. It is self-destructive to set tasks for oneself that are so difficult that one cannot bear the thought of them, and then to become bogged down in months and years of self-recrimination in which nothing is accomplished, guilt feelings become enhanced, and enjoyment is spoiled by the thought of the malignant task.

It is self-destructive to participate in the destruction of others. Is there a reader who has not borne the brunt of the unreasonable anger or drive to power of a parent or teacher or supervisor? Is there a reader who in turn as parent, teacher, supervisor, or *even friend* has not turned around and nagged, molested, been critical or nonsupportive of some human being who deserved or expected some greater warmth? Have you ever been fired, bereaved, failed an assignment, and then wondered why no one was available to share your suffering? Have you wondered whether an employee you have been insolent toward reported a failure, or did not cover up a mistake when the top boss came down on an inspection? Are you a disappointed lover or spouse who is concerned about the unexpected rage and striking out of a long-suffering mate? Maybe you were so mean and insensitive that your suffering was not only certain but also deserved!

Are you concerned about our country's war? Perhaps you feel public transportation is scandalously inadequate? Did the telephone company arbitrarily turn off your service and then charge you to restore it? Did an employee of some private company or governmental agency neglect your interest or abuse you when you needed service? Yes? Oh, you did nothing about it? You didn't sign a petition, or join a political club, or write to a newspaper, or ask to see the clod's supervisor? You are found guilty of the crime of self-destructiveness. Next case.

What about you and your job? You are underpaid? Too bad.

Your supervisor plays favorites? That's dreadful. The owner of the company is skimming off the profits and not paying taxes? Awful. Your boss shouts at you and humiliates you in public? Dreadful. You know that you're creative and you must do repetitive work? How ghastly! You wish you had more skills so that you can be assigned to that other fascinating department? It would be grand. Passed over for promotion? Tough. If these events have taken place and you have made no changes, you deserve it because you are either lazy, cowardly, or stupid. Oh, now I understand. You need security. The truth is that you are self-destructive.

By the way, how is your sex life? Are you having the kind of warm, vital relationship you have dreamed of since those wet-dreaming, grubby hand-pawing days of your uneducated, yearning adolescence? No? I see, your partner wasn't so hot and you told him (her) so in no uncertain terms! "Well, my beddytime pal tries so hard, but I like a good fight before I'll yield myself." "No, it isn't *that* way with me, but he wants to do that really dirty thing to me." "Well, everything else about our relationship is all right, but my wife isn't very sexual and I have a great big need to have my masculinity confirmed since I was a boy, so I'll drop her and get someone better." "My story is different. My husband is not patient with me. I know I've been married for *years,* but he is very critical and he is so impatient." "With *me,* I would feel like a slut if I ever let go. Really nice women don't move around and make all those disgusting noises." "My girl is very passionate, but it takes me forty-five seconds to climax, and she isn't satisfied; but I know that if she were normal she could climax twice with all that fooling around beforehand. Did I seek therapy? No, why should I? Besides, that's for sickies." "I don't need therapy. I need a loan. My wife is pregnant. She told me she just *knew* she couldn't get pregnant that time of the month."

Let's have a checkup on your feelings. "Why bother? I trust my feelings." Listen, I've been watching you. Your boss abuses you, your mate dumps on you, your friends kid you, and you never learned how to say "ouch." And as for you, yes, you, over there in the corner, when you get irritated, there is no stopping you. You and your loud voice and insensitive tongue. Just because your mother/father abused the family doesn't give you a license to cut everybody to shreds. Oh, you feel that this is a dog-eat-dog world and you don't want anybody nibbling at your bones? Well, just walk around with your hands guarding the family jewels because you're really well loved, you self-destructive character!

And, friend, how are you taking care of yourself? Exercise? "Got too many valuable things to do." Vitamins? "Nah, I eat a healthy diet of French-fried potatoes, Fritos, and pork chops." Overweight? "You have no idea how unhappy I am late at night." Relaxation? "I'm too tense." Sunshine? "Oh, boy, there is a carcinogenic compound that gives me a really marvelous tan without ever going out." Medical checkup? "Sure, next summer when I'm not so busy." Vague pain in the tummy? "Listen, those doctors really don't know anything. They can't be trusted." Which of these self-destructive idiocies are your proud possession? "Oh, I don't brush my teeth or wash my hands now after going to the bathroom because my father insisted on it years ago."

So, how do you handle money? Don't look away. You or your ever-loving are spending your most productive hours/days/weeks/months/years/decades earning it. Answer the question. "Well, my wife drove me into debts which are equal to over two years' earning before taxes. Cancel her credit cards? Oh, she wouldn't like that. Besides, she says I should have sex with her more often than once every two weeks." What's so terrible about that? "Well, I never liked her. Her style is so different from my own." You over there? "Oh, I lost my job because of embezzlement. My wife is so insecure and she really needed that grandiose house to live in. Me? It isn't so inappropriate for a fine fellow like me, either." Can I get into this? You see, I had this swell firm. It seems that I stole a great idea from my employer, who was really a crook in the way he handled his clients. Don't tell anyone, but my career-counseling firm went under because I started opening offices all over the East Coast while the recession was taking hold.

The economy was bound to turn around. What did my employees advise me? Listen, I'm smarter than anyone. Oh yeah, one of them did win a suit against me because I didn't want to pay him his vacation wages when I transferred him from one dummy company to another." "This conversation makes me feel edgy. It seems that I had all my money tied up in the market when everything went down. Funny thing, you know that broker who put me into Inter-Planetary Packaging? I never heard from him." Keep it up, fellas. Welfare is very popular. A few new cases won't be noticed. And as for you, madam, you may think that your daughter loves you because you give her everything she wants, but when her husband kicks her out on her expensively clothed rear you will be supporting her again and maybe a couple of emotionally starved grandchildren also. Self-destructive.

Speaking of grandchildren, I'd like to have a few words with you eager lovers. What's doing? "Well, I'm getting married because that's the only way I'll ever get her to bed." "Well, I don't want to be the only girl left unmarried on the block. Boy, you should hear my mother nag me about wanting grandchildren. Say, what's wrong about getting married because I'm lonely, pregnant, hard up, jealous, avaricious, guilt-ridden, passive, aggressive, sado-masochistic, dependent?" There is nothing wrong with any of these reasons for marriage except self-destructiveness.

"I'm none of those things, but I have one helluva time finding my mate. I don't know what I'm doing wrong. I advertise in a magazine that is sold on the newsstand. Lots of people can find out about me. I go to a bar which is really crowded. I know, I get stuck next to a creep all night and couldn't move even if I tried. I even sleep with everybody that I meet so I can really get to know them." "I'm different. I don't sleep with anybody I meet. I really have to know somebody very well before I'll do that." "As for me, I like to go out with lots of girls simultaneously. That way I can really compare them. True, I am a little tired after four nights of sex, but when the one comes along who is really meant for me I will really know." "You have it all wrong. You have to look at their sign. There was this dreamiest guy, but when I found out he was a Taurus—I'm a Leo—that really turned me off. You know how they mix!" "Well, astrology is all right, but my guy is going to have to be the right religion. You should have heard my mother when she heard that I went out with a Jew/Catholic/Protestant/Black/White/Redskin/Japanese." You self-destructive fool! You will deserve what you get or don't get.

By now you will have decided whether you are a self-destructive person. You may make decisions which prevent you from achieving happiness through emotional mistakes or through *poisoning the emotional environment in which you live.* I believe that most people are self-destructive even though they know better. Imagine that a friend were to take you firmly aside, sit you down, and say, "Look at yourself. If someone were to come to you and describe actions/feeling/talk like yours in this or that vital activity or important relationship, what would you say about him? Pretend that you are looking at yourself as an outsider." If the answer is that such a person is behaving against his best interest, that the effects he has on those he loves or needs or wishes the respect from are poor, then you, the reader, *lack emotional common sense.*

It is the writer's plan to help you toward self-understanding, to review many of the key areas in which self-destructiveness violates emotional common sense, and to alert you to recognize and change these important aspects of your behavior. Perhaps feelings you experience can improve. Hopefully the relationships you are now messing up will be more constructive. If, after reading the sections on avoiding self-destructiveness, you have changed in some ways but are still bogged down, unhappy, and unable to cope with important problems, then there will be a chapter explaining psychotherapy and some ways of selecting a competent psychotherapist.

In order to overcome your hangups and the various ways in which you torture yourself and some of the people you deal with, it is necessary to understand how you became self-destructive, to gain some insight into your needs and other characteristics, and to become more socially sensitive.

In the next two chapters we will review some of the common circumstances which lead to self-destructiveness. Then some pointers will be offered toward self-understanding (Chapter 4) and social sensitivity (Chapter 5). It is true that parents and society in general misshape us and point us down the road to self-destructiveness. It is also true that with greater self-understanding and social sensitivity you will be able to blame others and manipulate somewhat more successfully than before. Let me warn you, however, that *if you blame others you will remain the same insensitive, cruel, inefficient, self-destructive clod that you are now.*

The road to suicide, to the ultimate self-destructiveness, is lined with *hopelessness.* The road to emotional common sense, to productivity, to happiness, to self-esteem is paved with self-understanding, optimism, and a useful goal.

2 *Your Defective Brain*

Having read this far, you have likely reached the insight that you are self-destructive at least at times. Perhaps you may be depressed or pessimistic about the possibility of changing this unhappy, damaging state of mind. I believe that you need not be self-destructive but can make changes that will alter your behavior and thus change your feelings about yourself and the quality of the social and material world in which you live. Be courageous and read on.

In order to avoid or reduce self-destructiveness, you must know something about its origins. While a broad self-understanding might require considerable psychotherapy of a particular kind, some general knowledge of how people develop can be of aid to you in improving your lot in life.

The chief cause of self-destructiveness is the gross inefficiency of the human brain. This may come to you as a surprise, since you have been taught that the human brain is a marvel of complexity, that it has billions of cells, each intimately connected into ganglia, which serve the functions of rational thought, emotion, perception, coordination, etc. This statement is true, but it ignores the realities of life. The realities of life are that people slaughter one another by the tens of millions, most marriages fail, most children grow up to be neurotic, educational processes are chaotic, employment conditions are misery-provoking, loneliness is widespread, suicide is a frequent cause of death, and so forth.

Therefore, if you are to avoid emotional self-destructiveness you will have to admit that your brain is inefficient—specifically, that it leads to inaccurate conclusions. Further, you must accept the fact that your muscles, glands, and vital organs are maladapted to modern living. You will also have to concede that your feelings are not to be trusted, that they mislead you as to the nature of your relationships with the important people in your life. In addition, you will have to admit that your memory is faulty, that you don't remember what is convenient for you to forget, and you do remember many events and experiences which you would be better off to forget. It would be helpful if you realized that your judgment about people is poor and that your self-understanding is inadequate. To repeat: All of these defects which lead to self-destructiveness are due to the inefficiency of the human brain.

To avoid self-destructiveness you will have to undergo a process of self-understanding which will involve the slow undoing of many of the misconceptions, remembered injuries, and fallacious ideologies that you were taught or invented yourself. Subsequently, we shall see that some self-discipline also will be helpful. Yes, I said self-discipline, but that painful topic will be deferred till later.

At this point the reader should ask a sensible question: Are you not exaggerating? No, I am not exaggerating. I mean every word I have written. Nevertheless, you may persist, are there not worthy and even notable achievements of the human mind (read brain)? Of course there are. The technological/imaginative/ spiritual team which took man to the moon is a worthy example. Some of the writer's happiest moments were shared by thousands of others listening to performances of Beethoven, Schubert, Brahms, Mahler, and Mozart performed by a saintly man, Bruno Walter, leading the virtuoso musicians of the New York Philharmonic. The sculptures of Michelangelo, the paintings of Rembrandt, the formulations of Einstein, the plays of Shakespeare, the poetry of Milton, the courage and imagination of Freud are all examples of the human mind integrating and producing concepts of universal value. Why, then, the insistence that the human brain is inefficient and therefore the cause of self-destructiveness?

The reason is that while the brain does some things quite well, in the emotional area it is poorly designed. Most of us, for example, can learn the basic skills involved in walking, driving an automobile, playing baseball, typing, etc.—not well in all cases, perhaps, but satisfactorily. But when it comes to integrating our feelings, self-image, perception of people, anticipation of the future, and the other factors entering into emotional/social decisions, we often behave or experience in ways which are inappropriate or against our best interests. We evoke the hostility of others and display other attributes of emotional self-destructiveness. The remainder of this chapter will be devoted to some of the characteristics of the brain that contribute to the miserable human condition. We shall see that the brain is poorly adapted to the peculiar stresses of the modern environment.

Unfortunately, man's ability to formulate tools and work with abstractions has created problems at a far greater rate than his capacity to cope with new forms of stress, to be compassionate to others, and to foresee the adverse results of his actions. Consider the following accelerated rate of technological change. It is believed that the manufacture of well-made stone tools was initiated between three and four million years ago (L. H. Robbins, "Archaeology in the Turkana District"). The capacity to create fire at will probably evolved about forty thousand years ago, overcoming the widespread occurrence of toxic substances in plants which restricted their usefulness as food. Ground grain was probably first used as a source of food around 13,000 B.C. Pottery has been identified from about 8,420 years ago. The Old Kingdom of Egypt is generally considered to date from about 5,500 years ago (Leopold and Ardrey, "Toxic Substances in Plants . . .").

If we assume that the first, primitive pre-urban cultures started perhaps ten thousand years ago, man has utilized this tiny fraction of his evolutionary history to get himself into a mess from which a large proportion of us suffer because of the inadequacies of our bodies and minds to adapt to modern conditions (no, we have not yet reached the stage of civilization). But a moment ago in the evolution of our species, the problems of living for which we are largely adapted were considerably different from those of today. In a fascinating article in *Natural History* (May 1970), C. D. Darlington notes that our ancestors were differentiated into farmers, who domesticated crops, and pastoralists, who cultivated animals. He believes that the farmer's life "depended on his prudence and industry in handling the soil and crops . . . they are inbred, conservative and traditional, stubborn but peaceful. How different is the pastoralist! He is correspondingly attached to his animals, but his animals can move and usually have to move in search of pasture. He is therefore mobile, alert, and aggressive. He will steal the cattle and the women of his neighbors. Consequently, he is relatively outbred." Darlington notes that our forebears were also selected by the species they cultivated; only those with the wit to take advantage of the characteristics of selection of crops or animals would prosper.

Doubtlessly, food-raising differences were only a fraction of the factors that shaped our genetic heritage. Nevertheless, they illustrate the mental and physical characteristics necessary for survival too few generations ago to have been unbred during subsequent evolution. These characteristics are generally only partially relevant to cope with the complexities and problems of modern living. Julian Huxley has pointed out that cultural evolution proceeds at a rate hundreds of times that of biological evolution. Furthermore, genetic variability—i.e., individual differences—are required for the overall survival of the human species in changing environments. However, this implies that some individuals will have characteristics unsuited to the particular environment in which they live. For example, William Healy, a pioneer in community mental health, concluded that it is a "curious anomaly . . . when, in a given situation, such as that of restricted city life, great strength and activity appear as a liability for socialized conduct output, rather than an asset."

We have seen that mankind's biological capacity to adapt to changing circumstances lags far behind his capacity to create a new, complex, and stressful society.

The reader may object that it is society or our parents or our educational system that causes individuals to be maladaptive, crippled, hampered, or morally defective. This is wrong on two counts. In the first place it tends to remove individual responsibility for the results of one's own actions. It is my thesis that the world is pretty bad, but it could be better if we all used emotional common sense. Secondly, even if we accept the idea that external events exert a malign force on our lives, with a more effective brain we could forget what is crippling or misleading from the past and correctly relate to events as they are in the present. In the next chapter we shall discuss what are the kinds of information and emotional stimulation that are received by the brain, then misinterpreted, or retained long past the time they are useful.

A well-designed and correctly functioning brain would select only relevant stimuli, would correctly interpret them, would relate the perception to a correct image of the person's body and personality, and would elaborate the meaning, feelings, and response according to a correct, selective memory of the person's past. Let's see what really does happen.

The human nervous system did not develop as a unit. Rather, some parts were inherited relatively unchanged and other parts developed subsequently. The base of the brain, continuous with the spinal column, is physiologically very old and similar to that found in relatively primitive vertebrates—e.g., it exercises control over such metabolic functions as eating, breathing, and elimination. But it also shapes many of those responses we call emotions —i.e., anger, fear, sex, and so forth. This "brain stem" interacts with portions of the cerebral cortex, or covering, which in turn also developed at different stages of human evolution. Thus, our perception of the world, influenced by associations, conditioning, old memories, perceptions of our body and family, are in constant interaction with basic feelings, appetites, physiological conditions, and so on. The many centers and integrating mechanisms evolved at different stages of human evolution. Our reactions, then, are a mixture of fact, fiction, fantasy, and physiological functioning.

In addition to imperfect perceptions, there occurs imprecise coordination of various portions of the brain itself, such as lack of precise integration between the motor system, which controls overt actions, and bodily or autonomic functions which support life. This was attributed by Alfred Romer to the independent evolution of these two parts of the nervous system. It may be the basis for psychosomatic illnesses.

In addition to the immediate reaction of the various portions of the brain to one another, the brain stimulates various glands to secrete hormones. These substances in turn cause reactions, both immediate and delayed, which have subsequent effect on the brain's functioning.

All these factors, and others, not only lead us toward maladaptive reactions to the world but also cause individuals to resist change even when they are in psychotherapy (Parker, 1967).

For example, a concept is forming that hormonal effects *before birth* may have profound influences on our sexual behavior in maturity (Maggie Scarf in *The New York Times Magazine,* May 7, 1972, p. 30). It appears that the concentration of sex hormones of the developing fetus is crucial not only to sexual differentiation as a male or female but also to the development of what are considered masculine or feminine traits. While some of the studies are based on animals, there are also studies of human beings that indicate that prenatal maternal stress or inadvertent administration of hormones can prepare the brain for masculine or feminine sexual behavior at puberty, regardless of the apparent sex.

Also, some prenatal hormonal influence on intelligence and activity may occur. Thus, some of the so-called old wives' tales about frights and other effects of prenatal events on children might not really be fantasy. The importance of these findings is that some individuals might be programmed in terms of sexual behavior, amount of activity, intellectual patterns, etc., in ways that are unacceptable to the environment because of the discrepancy between their behavior and stereotyped expectations. These people have a special problem of development and identity, and their mothers are not completely to blame. The possibility of such prenatal influences should alert us to be more tolerant of our children and others entrusted to our care and not to be vindictive toward them because of their refusal to conform to our expectations. It also illustrates the relative inflexibility of our brain to cope with environmental demands.

Another way that hormones lead to inappropriate emotional responses is implied by Brady, who claimed that reactions may continue as long as seventy-two hours after the cessation of a traumatic stimulus. The brain continues to stimulate physiological reactions in the body, some of which are hormonal and thus have widespread effects. The body's continuing reactions long after a frightening or guilt-provoking event cause unrelated or trivial happenings, feelings, or ideas occurring subsequently to the painful experience to become associated with the physiological aftereffects of emotional traumata. Thus anxiety, terror, and the physiological after-effects of emotional traumata which we call fear and guilt become tied to irrelevant, harmless events, people, symbols.

We have seen that the brain cannot distinguish completely between the immediate effects caused by a particular event and the residual effects of previous events. An association is formed between present and past. This by itself would cause a blurring of experience, a combination of immediate and previous experiences. The situation is considerably worse than that. We also remember, in a highly distorted way, the events of childhood. What's so bad about that? If one has had a happy and constructive childhood, with a minimum of anxiety and constructive modeling from parents, the memory of one's life can form a complete pattern that adds richness, strength, and courage. Consider, however, what has happened in the life of you, the self-destructive reader.

There are many implications in the fact that children think and feel differently from adults. They organize and combine thoughts, fantasies, and feelings in distinctive ways. According to Jean Piaget and Barbel Inhelder, writing in *Psychology Today* (May 1970), the child is not only egocentric, considering his own point of view as the only possible one, but the "memory code" changes during development. This causes the memory of past events to change. What difference does it make that children feel, think, and combine differently than adults? The importance is that the images of self, parents, and the world in general become strongly connected with feelings. Furthermore, the child develops fantasies of himself, his parents, how he would like to be in the future, strange people and creatures, all with a heavy charge of feelings and drives toward action. Now, these images, fantasies, concepts, etc., consist of patterns and parts which are selected and combined in ways that are very different from grownups' ways. For example, they may consist of a mixture of bodily feelings, pleasant or unpleasant, and the image of part of oneself and part of one's parent. The vagueness and intensity of this mental structure is not communicated, understood, or remembered through the use of words. (With increasing maturity the formation of concepts and their organization become closer to that which we call adult.) Now, when the child has developed these mental structures, or "identification nuclei," as I have called them, they may influence him for a long time. His mother's rage, her description of him as a "bad boy," her sending him upstairs to a dark room, supperless, after a spanking, in a state of anxiety, anger, loneliness, hunger, reduced self-esteem, and hopelessness, all these create a condition which will haunt him for a long time. This combination of self-image, external environment, relationship to an important authority figure, and an angry, depressed mood can be brought back in times of fear, hallucinogenic drug use, illness, emotional stress, sickness, rejection, aloneness, darkness, etc. Further, this out-of-date combination of feeling about oneself and attitude toward the world can be manifested as a chronic state of malaise or sense of inferiority which affects school, employment, relationships with the opposite sex, choice of friends. The important point is that *it is not erased after the fact.* The inefficient brain keeps it as an influence on behavior long after it is irrelevant, even downright harmful.

If the above possibility is insufficiently frightening, consider the following. The same boy who has been emotionally brutalized goes to his room and develops a fantasy that goes something like this: "When I am older I am really going to be strong. No woman is going to push me around like that, *I am going to get even.* You wait and see." Here we have the identification nucleus of the domineering, sadistic man who has learned from his childhood suffering to feel vengeance, not compassion. He is the child-abuser, wife-beater, rapist, emotionally overbearing brute who serves as an active link in the world's chain of suffering—all of this based on the childhood fantasy of becoming strong enough to overcome his state of weakness and vulnerability and propelled into action long after he has reached a state of strength and independence. The brain is a magnificent organ, indeed!

Now let us consider the following early effects on learning and activity as discussed by Jerome S. Bruner. Although his study began with a consideration of children's learning blocks, remember that what he describes is really the beginning of neurotic inhibitions of creativity and productivity such as you yourself are suffering from. Bruner notes that the learning process in children combines *both* thinking about something and some form of action. Also, the *formation* of ideas is not separate from their *motivation* or *emotional* context. So, if a child is frightened by a dog and then is asked how a dog and a cat are similar, the fear associated with one will interfere with his capacity to relate it to a different, non-emotionally conditioned concept. Let's say that learning occurs in the context of fear of punishment for failure, or with the conditional reward of parental "love." In the future, the learning situation is not approached with a clear mind. Rather, extraneous anxieties or needs for reassurance become involved, with resultant poor performance.

Furthermore, by a process of assimilation, new events are related to what may be described by the author as a fear- (or other emotion-) accumulating concept. Bruner cites an example of a boy with a retribution-and-injury theme. His fearfulness and defensive attitude caused him to scan the environment and add many new objects to the concept "what will hurt me." As a result, the boy developed an especially subjective point of view instead of learning to deal with new events objectively.

These unfortunate attitudes of fearfulness or aggression, which assimilate many ordinarily non-emotional features of the world, are not erased. Quite the contrary, they flourish in the unconscious and affect perception and action trends in ways that are self-destructive. Thus, our miserable brain first creates illogical mental repression that makes us unaware that we are still nursing our wounds and grievances. Then it induces us to react in ways that create wounds and grievances in the people around us, and/or provokes them into further wounding and grieving us. Some brain.

The reader is undoubtedly aware of the concept of the unconscious, which is the keystone of Freud's psychoanalytic theory of personality. It is a complex phenomenon and incompletely understood, but essential to the understanding of how your brain misleads you. There are various reasons for attitudes and feelings to remain unconscious. The most familiar is repression—i.e., the effort to keep various ideas away from consciousness because they may lead to action. The action in turn will lead to danger, which is experienced as guilt or anxiety. Thus, to avoid temptation, the brain acts as though these wishes for sex, hostility, and so forth do not exist. Actually they show themselves indirectly through a variety of defense mechanisms which lead to partial gratification while we ordinarily are unaware of our own motives and also of the effect of our behavior on others.

Among the ways in which these earlier feelings of fear, anger, sex, and strong emotions are manifested are through displacement, projection, obsessions, compulsions, and hysterical conversions. All of these are forms of perception and behavior which put us into a state of self-delusion. We continue to kid ourselves that we are good little boys and girls being particularly obedient to our parents, rabbis, nuns, priests, teachers, and others concerned with our obedience and morality. For example, when we project, we attribute our own hostile wishes to another person, then attack or abuse him when it is ourselves who are the creators of the hatred. In displacement, for example, our employer picks on us, and we then find an excuse to spank the kid or yell at our spouse. In obsessions, an idea runs through our mind which partly relates to the forbidden wish and partly serves to confuse us that it exists. The compulsive action is an overt, repetitive, muscular action, which symbolically portrays our desires but may also delay genuine action. Finally, a hysterical conversion is a relatively constant change in our perceptions of the world, such as blindness or deafness or a muscular paralysis, representing the forbidden wish (which keeps us from seeing or doing what Mommy wouldn't like). Clearly a better designed brain would let us do what we felt like doing, after giving us a clear anticipation of the consequences.

You are not yet convinced that your brain is defective? Well, let me tell you this. The different ages of your life do not communicate very well. *What?* You remember that different parts of the brain evolved at different stages of mankind's evolution. In addition, different portions of the brain of the growing child mature at different rates. As a result, when certain portions are functioning—that is to say, learning, organizing, and coloring experiences—other portions are not yet ready to do so. Thus, the effective parts of the brain differ somewhat at different stages of development. Knapp believes that the parts which mature (myelinate) first are mostly related to emotional functioning, while those which develop later are related to rapid cognitive functioning. This may help to explain why the experiences and behavior of children are much more intense and "emotional" than those of many adults.

What is the practical effect of all this? It is very difficult for an adult to remember or to understand the experiences of his childhood. The style of understanding of the mature person does not "read" or translate very well the experiences of childhood. This helps to account for the fact that early experiences may be retained and influence our behavior, but they are not remembered in the sense of an accurate appraisal of the facts and their consequences.

No, don't ask for a brain transplant. That stranger on your left does not have a better brain than you do. What we can do is help you to use your own defective brain better by compensating for its weaknesses. Don't give up hope. Read ahead.

3 Your Childish Values

Let us consider your childish values. You may think of yourself as an adult. Well, if we look closely at the way you think, I'm afraid that many of your ideas developed when you were a lovable kid but not too perceptive—certainly not the independent thinker you are today.

From our point of view, the central facts of childhood are that children begin life weak and vulnerable, that they require consistent and extensive emotional warmth, that they communicate vaguely and think in terms of combinations of actions/feelings/ideas/images/combinations of inside and outside/unusual selection of parts to make up a whole, etc. The last point you have already mastered.

The newly born is completely dependent on the surrounding adults. Initial life in the world is not life-supporting as is life in the uterus. Cooperating adults are required who can comprehend the vague, insistent demands of the tiny infant. It is meaningful that among the criteria by which we evaluate the maturity of a civilization is the death rate of its infants.

The treatment received by the infant from the beginnings of life may have a profound effect on his values and philosophy. According to Karl Abraham, one of the most talented early followers of

Freud, in some cases "the person's entire character is under oral influence. . . . [Persons in whom sucking was undisturbed and highly pleasurable] . . . have brought with them from this happy period a deeply rooted conviction that everything will always be well with them. They face life with an imperturbable optimism which often does in fact help them to achieve their aims." Abraham states that for other people "there will always be some kind person—a representative of the mother, of course—to care for them and to give them everything they need. This optimistic belief condemns them to inactivity." An opposite, pessimistic attitude can also develop, which "goes back to disappointment of oral desires in the earliest years. . . . They consistently show an attitude towards life, and have a tendency to make the worst of everything and to find undue difficulties in the simplest undertakings." In this description of an early origin for basic expectations, we can see that the brain's frequent inability to distinguish between early experiences and current events can markedly affect our expectations and thus our behavior.

The specific reference to sucking is sometimes symbolic and sometimes an oral need profoundly affecting adult behavior. However, there is no question that the emotional quality of support and attention affects the child's self-esteem and his ultimate capacity to rid himself of a craving for affection. It also helps him develop a willingness to assume responsibility and cooperative social relationships. There are a number of ways in which the child's emotional life can be unsatisfying, which leads in turn to the feeling of chronic emotional deprivation in adulthood.

There can be direct cruelty to and neglect of the child. Unfortunately, such children may die, literally, of causes related to emotional starvation. A separate consequence is the tendency to develop furious feelings of hatred and desire for vengeance, with irrational hostility directed to other people. Another manner of handling a child's need for affection is to make it conditional on particular responses from the child. The child must be "nice," or obedient, or active, or quiet, and so forth. Thus, your attitude toward expressing your feelings or obedience or your sense of self-worth may easily have been crippled at an early age by parents who were good and affectionate to you only when you performed on cue, whether on the potty, the piano, or the podium. The child's vulnerability, his need for affection, for physical contact, for emotional security can also be made a hostage to the parental values. Think. How do you feel about cleanliness, scholastic attainment, professional status, political parties, sex, showing your anger, and other basics of life? The odds are that any deviation from the explicitly stated parental norm or, worse yet, their hidden beliefs, was threatened with loss of love, spanking, banishment, scorn, turned backs, or other examples of parental tenderness and competence. Not yet convinced? Try bringing home a homosexual partner or someone of a different race or religion. You will learn that your devoted parents are devoted primarily to their own social anxieties, prejudices, and drive to power.

Really, what did your parents need from you? They needed a child of whom they could be proud. This is not the total picture by any means, and we will discuss parental expectations and their consequences in the next chapter, on knowing yourself. How does a child cause his parents to be proud, and how is the growing mind molded to this end? A child causes a parent to be proud when he meets the parents' fantasies necessary to create a fine social image in the eyes of family, friends, and community.

The child's feelings of vulnerability and intellectual and emotional weaknesses are exploited to permit him to be molded according to the parents' needs. If the child senses that the parents are ridiculous, unfeeling, excessively demanding, selfish, unmindful of his needs, or plain spoilsports, he risks being "bad," rebellious, naughty, dirty, sinful, immoral, or other degrading things. He can be punished physically, isolated, scorned, threatened with hell, compared with more acquiescent peers, nagged, have other siblings treated as favorites, disliked, and suffer other forms of nastiness and abuse—all of this in the name of providing pride and pleasure for his parents.

Your parents want you to be a carbon copy, not of their own behavior but of their vague fantasies, ideals, fanaticisms, prejudices, and also those of their parents, teachers, clergy, political leaders, soap-opera writers, fictional heroes or heroines, media advertising directors, and other emotionally inadequate molders of values. The values that were implanted in you may have had their origins thousands of years ago in prehistory or in another country, or in the tortured mind of an emotionally disturbed person or cynical producer of movies/TV/pulp, or a hating, prejudiced cult leader. However, those values are now yours to shape your goals, your loves, your attitude toward employment and creativity, toward friends and associates, toward politics, civil affairs, neighbors, and military service. Oh, yes, they are also yours to influence your children, evaluate your employees, relate to your dates or mate, select your neighbors, vote, choose entertainment, decorate your house, select your clothing, pick your courses and career, spend your leisure time, etc.

Are you going out on a date? Has your partner the right height, hair color, education, occupation, social background, personality, sexual attitude, preference for entertainment, attitude toward marriage, children, and neighborhood? Can he/she mix nicely with your friends and family? Does he/she vote for the right party, have the right attitudes toward war, radicals, welfare, crime in the streets, left-wingers, right-wingers? Politics is important, but why associate such an important value with selecting a mate?

Do you really believe that you have a rational attitude toward politics? Do you believe that yours is the only intelligent approach to the variety of international and intranational problems facing our nation? In an article in *The New York Times* (April 23, 1972) Eugene V. Rostow asked the question: "Eight Foreign Policies for the United States—Which Is Yours?" He indicated that "since 1945, there has been acute dissonance in the nation between what we thought and what we did in the name of foreign policy of the United States." Is it likely that there are eight intelligent ways of conducting the foreign policy of the United States? Consider only the listed alternatives: (1) The world-government utopians; (2) the isolationists; (3) the balance-of-powerites; (4) the all-out anti-Communists; (5) the men of *Realpolitik;* (6) the pacifists; (7) the Communists; (8) the missionaries of democracy. It would not take much investigation to detect the similarities between these political values and expectations of authority and the handling of angry feelings within the family. Some people become isolationists, some rebel against generally accepted values, some look to priests and outside agencies, some like open struggle, and so forth. The next time you cast your vote or start a political struggle, please ask yourself: Am I an intelligent, well-informed, rational, well-meaning citizen, or am I an angry, frustrated incompetent, continuing the old family fight? Then I suggest that you ask yourself carefully and with complete reflection: Is this point of view in my own interest today or tomorrow? Is this amount of violence (or passivism) necessary or realistic? Is that group out there as malevolent as I imagine them to be (like the —— when I was a kid)? Is it intelligent to put that group into a corner just because today my group has a monopoly on power? Am I that deprived that I must take the last bit of dignity and material well-being from somebody else, or blow them up, or imprison them? If the answer is yes, you are probably acting out neurotic feelings of injustice and rage emanating from unkindness in your childhood and engaged in transferring your anger to somebody else.

This is positively not an exaggeration. We shall describe later the various kinds of family atmospheres and their influence on how we express our feelings, including ways of handling anger and selecting irrational targets.

Let us return to your childish values. Are you considering marriage or have you taken the plunge? In *Sexual Behavior* (January 1972) Dr. John F. Cuber has described "Sex in Five Types of Marriages." Make sure that your values match those of your mate. What are you talking about? Sex is just plain healthy fun. Oh, no it's not. It's part of a deep-seated need for affection. Oh, no, it's plain disgusting. No, it's a spiritual expression. This quarrel hasn't even scratched the surface. Dr. Cuber has described five different adult values that also reflect values developed in childhood concerning sex, anger, and how to solve conflicts. "Conflict-habituated couples" value a high amount and intensity of conflict. "The conflict-habituated apparently do not make the more conventional connections which popular stereotypes embrace among love, congenital interaction, and sexual gratification." Then he considers the "passive-congenial." These are people who do not place a high value on sex but are "relatively quiet orderly couples who for the most part do the things they are supposed to do, like raising children, attending to their jobs and community responsibilities." What does that have to do with a good sex partner? Nothing, believe me. "Devitalized" couples once had an enjoyable sexual experience. Some of the wives were noted for being more preoccupied with parenthood than with spousehood and now resolve their sexual conflicts through responsibility to the children. Devitalized marriages are experienced by people who "really believe it to be an appropriate mode for the middle years." Appropriate for whom? As a model for growing children? The "vital" marriage, on the other hand, is characterized by couples who "are deeply involved psychologically in each other and in the aspirations and values which the mate holds." In short, these people are living in the present and are not being guided by childish values. This is also true for that even deeper involvement called the "total" marriage in which "the vitality extends to virtually all important life foci." While there are differences in attitudes toward fidelity (greater liberality in the "vital" type) between these two types of mates, they seem to have liberated themselves from inappropriate ties to the attitudes of their childhood. Or putting it differently, their parents did not play on their vulnerability or squelch their individuality so that they could not use and enjoy their souls and bodies as they saw fit.

We have seen some instances in which values developed early in life shaped such complex attitudes as the proper way to express anger and sexuality in marriage. Let us look more closely at how family attitudes influence how you think long years after the fact. It would be rare for a child to be told that he could express any thought he wanted, that any feeling is honest, that any expression deserves a serious and courteous response, a loving concern from his parents. But don't fall into the error of thinking that all parents are the opposite. Parental styles concerning the expression of feelings in a household are variable.

In the chapter on emotional pain we will review the ways in which parents teach their children that to be a feeling human being is unacceptable in their household. We can anticipate this by noting that there are three kinds of homes that will influence the way in which you fight with your mate. Therefore, if you are planning to marry, read this carefully so that you can pick a spouse whose technique of expressing anger is similar to yours. If you have already made the plunge, you can decide whether you and your ever-loving have come from the same type of background when it comes to handling your conflicts in a similar, compatible way. Otherwise, you are in trouble and will have to take special care to avoid serious and damaging confrontations.

Some homes condition their children to be "nice." What this really means is that the children are taught to value propriety and the illusion of good will over the reality of unreasonableness, frustration, anger, emotional deprivation, and intense sexual feelings. You are taught that "nice" children do not act in certain ways. This may be translated to mean the following: "Since I the parent am stronger than you, and since I am not interested in your feelings and individuality, and since the religious and/or social code in which I was raised is more important than my relationship with you, my disobedient and therefore bad child, you must conceal your feelings; you must not raise anxiety in me concerning my own weaknesses, neuroses and hypocrisy, but rather you must learn to be 'nice.' "

Other homes will teach you that the best way to solve a problem is to be "abusive." The valued, successful person is the one with the loudest voice, the shortest temper, the swiftest slap, the most exaggerated insult. The child in such a home is taught that the happiest way to achieve good human relationships, particularly in the intimacy of the home, is to engage in a verbal/physical shoving match. In this way, through survival of the fittest (read nastiest), the correct emotional atmosphere will evolve in which all parties will learn to work together harmoniously. I have no objection to two bullies mating and thus keeping other innocent parties from marrying them. Such people are likely to treat each other in the insensitive, brutish way they were exposed to. However, when such a person reared in an "abusive" household relates to one with a different background, the latter never knows what hit him. Fortunate is he (or she) who discovers early in a relationship that the fighting style of his mate is to meet the slightest challenge with the emotional equivalent of an uppercut.

A more subtle form of emotional crippling is the "emotionally depriving home." This household does not teach its children to be nice or warm or abusive. The parents are basically unreactive, and the growing child's normal responses, his warmth, frustration, love, manipulations, learning, are not reacted to. Whether it is love or hurt feelings, the child learns that his feelings are of no value. As a result he experiences rejection and ultimately turns off his feelings in order to spare himself the humiliation of being emotionally ignored. Among such parents' motives are exploitation of their children (No, Virginia, not all parents are Santas at heart), avoidance of emotional responsibilities, and a compulsive belief that the children must always play the same dependent, childish role. As a result, the child learns to value being "cool"— i.e., non-responsive and detached. Such people avoid others who are more emotionally expressive and are a source of frustration to someone who wants a good interchange, whether loving or fighting. In fact, for really self-destructive people, the need to engage such a withdrawn person can be especially entrancing but will probably lead only to disappointment.

How about childish religious values? I know one person whose priest yelled at him from the privacy of the confessional, within earshot of others, that if he continued to masturbate he would become insane. Please don't accuse me of being anti-Catholic. The Orthodox Jews have the pleasant custom of the mother slapping her daughter on the inception of menstruation. Their men believe that women should be isolated in a separate part of the synagogue and not be approached during menstruation or even afterward until they have had a ceremonial bath—as if Jewish mamas didn't keep themselves and anything under their control as aseptic as an operating room. The Protestants are not always accepting of little derelictions either. I remember trying to take the director of religious education of a Presbyterian church to a nice restaurant in the vicinity of the pitiful little town in which we both worked. She refused even to enter because adjacent to the dining room was a bar, and she was teaching the children in her care not to drink. Result: We went to a local greasy spoon. Subsequently, she married a local man with a drinking problem (like her father) who beat her up.

Another area in which the child is frequently assaulted is in being trained to assume a particular sexual or social role. If he is a male, then he must be dominant, emotionally unresponsive, sexually assertive (assuming that he isn't impotent from fear of insanity, hairy palms, hell, castration, having his hands burned, etc.). He is taught by his mates to "score" and by his sexually frustrated mother to treat women like the Virgin Mary. His school insists that he conform in dress, deportment, grades, while his peers want him to play, to fight, and to resist the feminizing atmosphere of the school. His parents want him to keep up with the Joneses, restraining his needs, but they can't be bothered either to explain the values of conformity or to tell the Joneses to shove it.

If you are a girl, from the beginning you are given a doll, a baby carriage, and a toy stove that will electrocute you if you touch it with wet hands. In school did you go to shop or to cooking classes? Unless you were raised in a really healthy sexual environment such as those experienced by certain pigmented minorities, you are taught that the genital area must be held more inviolate than Fort Knox.

That's not the end of the story. Your mother will then either send you powdered and lipsticked on dates before you can spell sanitary napkin, or keep you locked up after seven-thirty for fear that some genital stimulation will ruin you worse than the Wreck of the Hesperus. Now, Daughter, remember this: No man will respect you if you let him touch you, and I won't respect you if you are not married at twenty-one.

If you are now depressed, cheer up. Beginning in the next chapter you will be taught how to understand yourself, to avoid self-destructiveness, and to learn how to give up childish values—in short to put your defective brain to work for you.

4   *Toward Self-Understanding*

I trust that the reader has now satisfied himself that he must concentrate on avoiding self-destructiveness. This chapter and subsequent ones are designed to give you some tools necessary to increase satisfaction from life and reduce self-destructiveness.

In this chapter we will deal with the basic structures of personality. Individuals differ considerably in some characteristics and have much in common in others. By having respect for both the differences between individuals as well as the basic drives and needs shared by all, you will be more capable of understanding yourself and those you come in contact with. You will insist that others treat you as an individual, and you will be aware of the needs and sensitivities of the important people around you. The next chapter aims to educate you in some ways of being more socially sensitive. Then you will be on the road to both more cordial interpersonal relationships and also to knowing which individuals bring out those strong discomforts you experience. I will discuss the various specific unpleasant feelings you want to overcome and various specific problem areas in which you may well have demonstrated your lack of emotional common sense.

The road to self-understanding commences with some key concepts: adaptation, constitution, and temperament. These ideas will help you to understand the vocabulary and grammar of your emotional life and those who are important to you.

The key to emotional understanding is the idea of *adaptation*. By adaptation is meant the way in which people cope with reality. We all have a certain anatomical structure and physiological reactions. In addition to these we gain some idea of ourselves, our skills, attitudes, and so forth, which in turn influence the choices we make as we cope with life. The entire process of survival, particularly as it is characterized by a unique pattern characteristic of a person, may be described as adaptation. Some people adapt to reality successfully—that is, they are productive, happy individuals maintaining good relations with others. Each has certain traits and manners of perceiving and reacting that bring success and happiness. Other individuals, because of either poor biological structure, repeated blows to their psyche, or faulty guidance and conclusions concerning reality, are unable to cope with reality. Their patterns have resulted in those defects of adaptation that we call psychosis, criminal behavior, or escapism through drug abuse.

The second concept you must learn is that of *constitution*. According to R.M. Goldenson in *The Encyclopedia of Human Behavior*, this is defined as "the relatively enduring biological make-up of an individual, in part due to heredity, and in part to life experience and environmental factors." It can be seen that the supporting functions of strength and energy, health and reactivity, which are most important contributors to adaptation, are included in constitution. The lucky person with a strong constitution has endurance, health, resistance to disease and stress. He faces difficulties without collapsing or developing psychosomatic illnesses or emotional discomforts. The person with a weaker constitution is vulnerable to illness, is unable to perform under stress without fatigue, ulcers, heart attacks, emotional discomfort, etc. It is important that you evaluate your constitution, improve your health where possible, and then set definite limits beyond which you will not force yourself to go except in emergencies.

You may be skeptical because most of the popularizers of psychological phenomena have stressed the mental aspect of adaptation. This approach is one-sided and thus partially incorrect. You will be severely hampered if you believe them and ignore the body which carries your valuable psyche. When was the last time you enjoyed sex while having a toothache or spoke comfortably with your supervisor with a full rectum? Mental functioning requires a capable body if you are to carry on. A Beethoven or Helen Keller (deaf), a Steinmetz (crippled), or a Franklin Roosevelt (paralyzed) are exceptions. These magnificent human beings had courage and stamina to compensate for the frailties of their bodies.

We are now in the process of helping you to assess your own weaknesses and start a self-development program.

Goldenson defines temperament as "a general term for emotional make-up, including characteristic energy level, moods and mood changes, intensity and tempo of reactions to people and situations." Temperament can also be considered as aspects of behavior by which all persons can be described and which also contribute to the differences between people—traits that are least affected by the physical and social environment during development. Any given characteristic may last a lifetime or may slowly change until the person in this particular regard is vastly different from the way he was when he was born.

It is useful now to consider the basic emotional reactions with which we are born. Please pay close attention to what follows. The descriptions of the various temperamental traits will be useful in helping you to understand yourself and others and how your reactions are relatively unique and different from those around you. Thus, in selecting a mate, choosing a job, picking friends, etc., your temperament is part of the equipment with which you adapt. And if you are a parent or teacher, you will approach the children under your care with greater sympathy for their individual differences because you will be *able to recognize them.*

The following list of *temperamental characteristics* was obtained by a team of child psychiatrists (A. Thomas *et al*, in *Temperament and Behavior Disorder in Children*). Their findings are extremely important: Children have unique patterns—i.e., they differ from each other—*from birth*. The behavioral apparatus with which you and your children came into the world was unique from the beginning. The implications are profound. The child is not totally shaped by his parents, nurses, teachers, siblings, etc. The child is not infinitely malleable clay to be pushed and pulled according to the unsympathetic demands of unaccepting parents. Rather, the child has a drive to live and do things his own way. When the parents support, guide, educate, and correct in a warm, kindly way, the child flourishes, gains confidence, and enjoys a *joie de vivre*. When, however, the parents and schools try to mold the child to fit the preconceived notions of how he should act, when they shove here, press there, shape over yonder, then the child responds with resistance, compliance, and unhappiness.

Here, then, is a list of temperamental characteristics with which we come into the world. Their relevance to adult behavior is noted.

1. *Activity level*. Individuals differ in their amount of activity, the pace with which they function, and how often they perform muscular acts. Children vary in their response to bathing, being fed, etc., while adults differ from being very inactive to tearing around all over the map.

2. *Rhythmicity*. This means regularity or predictability. Although adults are more predictable than infants in sleeping and eating habits, one must often have to cope with individuals whose pacing and regularity of habits and activities are different from one's own.

3. *Approach or withdrawal*. This describes the child's or adult's initial attitude toward new situations, such as people, food, procedures, etc. Some individuals are quite reluctant to confront anything new, while others are eager for a change of scene and faces. Taken to the extreme, this trait can lead people to develop into politicians or explorers, club presidents or wallflowers.

4. *Adaptability*. We can't always choose our environment—particularly not our associates or teachers. Thus, we must become

alert to our own ability to change when we have to cope with a new situation as well as the ability of the other party to accommodate himself to our own needs.

5. *Intensity of reaction.* People differ in the amount of energy they put into a reaction. This trait differs from 1 because it does not refer to the overall general pattern of energy or effort but to what happens in any individual act. Consider the difference between the phlegmatic, wilted-lettuce-leaf handshake and the Bull of the Pampas who sends you to your local chiropractor!

6. *Threshold of responsiveness.* How much of a stimulus or poke is necessary to cause a person to spring (or drag himself) into action? Consider the difference between the light sleeper and the log, between the person who jumps up with fists raised when someone looks cross-eyed at him and the indolent guy who can be stepped on without objecting.

7. *Quality of mood.* This is listed as 7 but ought to be close to the top of the list, since it is the aspect of our life which often concerns us most: how much pleasant, joyful, friendly behavior there is as contrasted with unpleasant, crying, and unfriendly behavior. This assessment, in yourself and those around you, should give some indication of the balance of destructiveness to emotional common sense you are experiencing or expressing.

8. *Distractibility.* The goal-orientedness of a person is a key characteristic in determining whether he is considered reliable, dependable, and likely to succeed in his chosen profession. Some children cry until they are picked up or until they are fed. Similarly, some people fight doggedly to their goal, while others fall by the wayside. As you plan your career or volunteer for assignments, consider your distractibility, because it might mean the difference between success and failure, no more and no less.

9. *Attention span and persistence.* In a related way, children sometimes will continue to play at a certain activity regardless of Mother's interference or they may voluntarily give it up in exchange for something else to do. The persistent child or adult may continue even in the face of opposition. The opposite type may

cease at the slightest reprimand or suggestion. Some small children persist in trying to stand up regardless of how often they fall; others give up at the first bruise. This trait can be useful or harmful, depending on the consequences. Obviously persistence can be enjoyed or hated, according to whether you are the subject or the target, the successful plodder or the outraged mother.

Keep these traits in mind, because they form the skeleton for all other activities in life and seem quite relevant to the adult's self-understanding and his evaluation of the people around him. Drs. Thomas, Chess, and Birch point out that children (and of course adults) develop generally under conditions of dissonance (lack of harmony) between their temperament and the demands of the world. Demands which are consistent with the person's capacities and characteristics result in mastery of varied kinds of situations. On the other hand, demands that the developing child or adult cannot meet are *stressful*. Subsequently we will point out some of the symptoms of *stress* so that you can recognize when you are under pressure and can learn to master or avoid it. If you are a parent and want to study these findings so that you can directly evaluate your child and learn how to cope with a "difficult" or particularly "persistent" child, I recommend that you go directly to this volume or to *Scientific American* (1970, pp. 22, 102–109).

Let us now discuss *basic needs*. While different psychologists have devised varying lists of basic needs, the idea that we will use here is a simple one. A need is something that is required from the world, something that we cannot easily provide for ourselves. If we use a biological model of needs, the human being needs oxygen, food, and water. We cannot provide these from within our own body. In the case of psychological needs, we require certain kinds of responses or feelings from people.

As individuals develop, they can become more independent if these basic needs are fulfilled. Otherwise we may experience scarring or deprivations which are hard to overcome.

The basic psychological needs required for healthy functioning are (1) love; (2) security and dependency; (3) sex; (4) recognition; and (5) companionship. People develop in ways that make them require a different intensity of these feelings from others. Since the purpose of this book is to enhance your personal emotional common sense, you will have to assess first your own intensity of needs and then that of those people who are important to you.

Love. This feeling of being wanted and cared for is one of the most central issues of life. Being loved is necessary for life in its earliest phases. Infants separated from their homes, placed in institutions where they are well taken care of so far as their physical needs are concerned but emotionally neglected, become apathetic and *often die.* To have developed in a loving atmosphere is to have a running-leap advantage in life. It is to experience value and self-confidence, to expect warmth, to seek a mate with expectation of success, and to be able to look forward and not backward. To grow up and not to feel loved is to be condemned to look backward with regret, to feel insatiable, to expect rejection and then enter into maneuvers which invite it and lose love. To have experienced significant amounts of love is to develop the confidence to overcome obstacles in your personal life and to weather temporary conflicts in your intimate affairs. When love has been received, it can be expressed and offered generously. Thus, to have no one to love or to love one who will not accept and reciprocate is among the most painful of experiences.

Security and dependency. Everybody needs the feeling that in time of trouble there is someone there to help, to care, to patch up the wounds. A violation of the child's security, for example, by the death or disappearance of a parent, lengthy separation from home through illness and hospitalization, or grossly inconsistent behavior by the parents makes him feel that the world is unreliable. The child becomes excessively dependent on his own resources, perhaps even withdrawn. The idea of disappointment and unexpected lack of support becomes haunting. Instead of being forgotten, this fear remains uppermost on the mind. A person may then look for relationships in which dependency is the most important consideration, eliminating the opportunity of satisfying other needs, or may avoid people and intimacy to a large extent in order not to be left alone again.

Sex. People probably differ more in their actual desire and means of obtaining satisfaction than in any other need. The ability and wish to have sexual satisfaction is observed even in infants. To be frustrated in this need is an invitation to anger, distractibility, and reduced self-esteem. The shaping of the sexual response is subjected to all kinds of pressures from the family, school, community, media, advertising, religion, etc. Some individuals cannot accept their sexuality at all; others set up very rigid constraints before they permit themselves to experience sex. Still others express their desires so extensively that it may be said that sex is the most important determinant of their way of life.

Recognition. It is important to people to belong somewhere, to feel that they play a definite role in society, that they are valued for their contribution. For some individuals, the idea of being part of a family—that is, the father or mother—is extremely important, and few other needs for connection are experienced. Others find satisfaction in being part of a large organization—for example, a big company or one of the armed forces. This is a form of *recognition.* Some people want to stand out as leaders or be famous. This is a form of dependency on others that can be very strong.

Companionship. Loneliness is experienced by many people as the most feared state of mind. Unless there is somebody *there for them,* then they become extremely troubled, unable to function, and likely to make poor decisions in a variety of areas. To have a companion is to feel valuable, to be able to share feelings and gain advice. As children grow up, many of their favorite activities can be performed only in the company of others. To be rejected is to feel worthless as a person and not to have fun. This state of mind is continued into adulthood, and there are many advantages to having the need for companionship fulfilled by cordial people.

The list of *basic needs* emphasizes what we *want* from the world. The list of *basic drives* stresses what we would like to *do to* the world. People are not only demanding and not only reactive to what is done to them. We create activity. We try to do things that are satisfying or new or creative. Perhaps some of these drives are not even learned but are built into the nervous system as our guarantee of survival. The list of basic drives which I am offering is (1) curiosity; (2) power; (3) productivity; (4) growth.

1. *Curiosity.* The quest for newness can be a most interesting and satisfying part of life. It is a basic drive, one which we have inherited from our primate forebears. As Harlow puts it (1953), "even young monkeys learn to solve simple and complex mechanical puzzles proficiently when motivated by manipulation or exploration alone." Surely human beings are not less curious than monkeys. This drive has taken us to the moon and the bottom of the ocean. Unless, of course, humans had parents who stifled their curiosity and were too impatient or uninformed to coach, guide, and permit this free direction of energy.

2. *Power.* The drive for power is practically equivalent to the written history of this sad world. What is history besides the recorded misdeeds of kings and dictators and the struggle of various classes to control or resist being controlled? One of the chief contributions of the Viennese psychiatrist Alfred Adler was pointing out that the adult drive for power and superiority evolved from the "inferiority complex." The child is obviously vulnerable before the assaults of parents, teachers, and bullies within and without the family. Frequently we develop the *goal* of overcoming weakness through being superior to others. Adler warns, however, in *What Life Should Mean to You,* that while "the striving for superiority is behind every human creation . . . the only individuals who can really meet . . . the problems of life . . . are those who show in their striving a tendency to enrich all others. . . ."

3. *Productivity.* Most people integrate their drives toward curiosity and power into a wish to be productive, to make something valuable which the world or special people can share, see, hear, or otherwise appreciate. When somebody is bedridden or in a situation in which his contribution is minimal, or nobody cares,

then the feeling of self-worth is diminished. Thus, it becomes vital if one's occupation, marriage, or social life is not satisfying to develop interests, hobbies, or other skills which can compensate for the drabness of a situation. This is particularly important for the housewife who may have had it "up to here" with the tedium and routine of domestic living. It is also true of individuals whose careers are at that stage where there is little satisfaction.

4. *Growth.* It has been pointed out by the psychologist Abraham H. Maslow in "Deficiency Motivation and Growth Motivation" that there are different drives or motives in people, depending on whether their drives are those of deficiency or those of growth. Deficiency drives are those which fulfill such deficiencies as basic needs. Only when these needs are largely met can individuals seek to achieve enhanced personal growth in many significant areas. The concept of self-actualization refers to the capacity to be spontaneous, to be easily expressive, to see reality without reference to one's own needs, to create, to identify with many others. To achieve self-actualization even means to be somewhat independent of others, because one's basic needs do not require excessive fulfilling from people. Individuals with a drive toward growth extend their personalities and experiences in a variety of ways without neurotic fear of the consequences.

We are now ready to consider the most interesting aspect of self-understanding—the idea of *personal identity,* or who you are. There are many ways of regarding this sense of self—for example, one's *body image* (picture of the physical person and his abilities), *basic attitudes* of assertion or compliance, the *social role* one plays, and the degree of *self-esteem.*

Our *sense of self* is determined in childhood in large part on the basis of how we are treated and how we see others. The process of observing parents, siblings, peers, teachers and trying to act like them is called *identification.* It is sometimes a means of avoiding anxiety, since we hope to avert punishment through being like the other person—i.e., taking those characteristics he or she seems to value. Another determinant of our identification is *how we are treated.* The child who is scorned, punished, isolated, abused, criticized begins to see himself as valueless, inadequate, dirty, hateful, harmful, etc. It is also possible to develop a self-concept with excessive feelings of superiority.

Part of the sense of identity is the *body image,* or what we think we look like. There are impressive deviations between what a person thinks he looks like and how others regard him or her. The most attractive and desirable person can be conditioned to see himself as ugly, distorted, and ungainly. Conversely, individuals who would be generally regarded as unattractive can defend against this through narcissism (an exaggerated sense of the beauty of one's body). Unfortunately, self-image is conditioned by the messages all around us, that certain body shapes, hair color, complexions, and so on are more desirable than others. Bust sizes, body proportions, facial features, and so many others can be given exaggerated importance and thus cause a person to relate to others in a highly distorted way.

Still another aspect of the sense of identification is the *basic attitude* or role in life. This was defined by my friend and mentor, Zygmunt A. Piotrowski, in *Perceptanalysis:* "as definite tendencies, deeply embedded in the subject and not easily modified, to assume repeatedly the same attitude or attitudes in dealing with others when matters felt to be important and personal are involved." Piotrowski defines the three main roles as follows: *Self-assertiveness*—"A deep-seated need for self-reliance and spontaneous activity, confidence in one's capacities, the initiation of activities, and the pursuit of personal goals without psychological dependence upon other people." *Compliance* is "the need to lean on someone psychologically stronger than himself whom he can implicitly trust to assume ultimate responsibilities, and under whose protective and benevolent wing he can display his full initiative, imagination, and activity." Finally, the *indecisive* or *blocked* person experiences "an inability to reach a final decision and to act forcefully and consistently when it becomes necessary to find a new way of handling a vital life problem."

One last concept you must learn in your struggle against self-destructiveness and toward emotional common sense is the idea of *self-esteem*. The worst gift that parents can offer their child is the continuing thought that he or she is no good, valueless, harmful, or unimportant. We have already seen that how we are treated becomes an important part of our sense of identity.

The value we place on ourselves will determine our success in any social or competitive area of life. Self-confidence, or high self-esteem, is often the difference between vocational success and failure, even when experience and ability are equal to others'. Surely, our choice of mate, kind of job, approach to education, and choice of career will be determined by how much value we place on ourselves. While it is possible to devalue oneself to the point of self-destruction, it is also possible to attempt tasks and gain companions or a mate which are unsuitable because it is not possible to accomplish the task or enjoy the relationship. Thus, the most difficult problems are, first, to estimate realistically what we are worth, then to exercise the self-discipline to improve our sense of self-esteem, and, finally, to select a variety of goals which are realistically attainable.

You have now some of the tools necessary for self-appraisal. The next task is to achieve some understanding of the social world in which you live.

In George Bernard Shaw's *Pygmalion* Liza Doolittle says to Colonel Pickering: "You see, really and truly, apart from the things anyone can pick up (the dressing and the proper way of speaking, and so on), the difference between a lady and a flower girl is not how she behaves, but how she's treated. I shall always be a flower girl to Professor Higgins, because he always treats me as a flower girl, and always will; but I know I can be a lady to you, because you always treat me as a lady, and always will."

5   *Toward Social Understanding*

You have now learned some of the internal factors in your personality. Since most feelings and attitudes develop in a social context, it is important to understand the structure of the social world as well. Lack of harmony between inner and outer milieus is a primary cause of stress. Part of the cause of self-destructiveness is not being able to select and/or create the kind of environment which will meet your needs and bring out the best and happiest part of your personality. Also, to participate in a suitable ambiance is to develop strength and security and thus be able to protect oneself against those critical unsatisfying relationships which have been cutting one down.

It is vital that you evaluate your *style of life* and, having done so, make the appropriate decisions to render it more satisfying. You will develop the capacity to look clearly at the people around you, those you work for, those who have been your models, your spouse or fiancé, or the teachers of your children. The style of life is an important component of how people act. It is a linkage between your inner world (as discussed in the previous chapter) and the demands of reality. It is a prominent personality complex which is hard to change.

Style of life is the kind of adaptation that people make, the compromises between their physical and mental capacities and the world they live in, which organize their behavior and provide some balance between gratification and discomfort. As Alfred Adler stated it in *The Science of Life*, the style of life is a way of describing the unity of a person's life, specifically the way he has learned to resolve his problems of early life, and his techniques for reaching goals. Past, present, and future congealed in the details of daily living!

In assessing your life style and those of others you deal with, I suggest that we use age and attitude toward material *necessities* as a convenient starting point. People tend to fall into at least three separate categories. For example, it seems reasonable to categorize a young child as primarily a *consumer*. He generally produces nothing of value. As the child matures, he may take a part-time or seasonal job, and the balance tips gradually toward becoming a producer. When he matures, becoming economically self-sufficient, particularly when living away from the family in which he grew up, we may consider a person to be a *producer*.

What about the housewife? I consider a woman, or man for that matter, who runs a household, raises children, and generally makes it possible for someone to earn a living to be very useful. Perhaps the term *maintainer* would be appropriate. A person who stays at home without responsibility, regardless of age, would be considered a consumer. You think *parasite* is a better word? I'm not in the mood for a fight.

In this vein, the large number of institutionalized individuals— for example, criminals, mental-hospital patients, etc.—are, from the viewpoint of their current life styles, consumers. This would include a certain number of persons who float around the country from pad to pad. They survive because of the extra material wealth of this country (housing, food, clothing) which they consume without being producers—i.e., offering something of value in exchange for a wage.

The last major category includes criminals, hoodlums, drug pushers, etc. These I consider *destroyers*. They destroy others' economic necessities and well-being while producing nothing of value.

Social attitudes represent another way of regarding life style. Some individuals live by themselves and seem to have little need of others or to tolerate them poorly if at all. Let's call them *isolates.* Other people function socially with comfort but can tolerate moments when they are alone or with large groups. They are *companions.* Finally, there are those who absolutely require one or two individuals to relate to, often in an emotionally needy way. They are very uncomfortable without such a person and make many decisions on the basis of whether it will alienate those on whom they depend. The term *clutcher* comes to mind.

Now let us consider the *location* where you live. This will include your city, neighborhood, block, and actual living quarters. To a large extent one's economic resources will determine one's life style. Unless you wish to risk a jail term for fraud and the change of category from producer to consumer, it is no use to rent a Park Avenue apartment on an East Third Street salary. However, there may be some affluent individuals who by choice will select a life style that is less materialistically oriented than the maximum they can afford.

At the opposite extreme is the unfortunate person who is forced to live in surroundings that are dangerous, impoverished, and poorly served by the community. Such persons' incapacity for entertainment, having others come to their homes, free access to the outside world, peace of mind, health, and daily surroundings will put a severe strain on their mental well-being and could certainly result in feelings of humiliation, degradation, and ultimately rage or apathy.

The location also affects your style of life through the *values* of the community. You might select directly the actual location in which you live because the community shares particular values or indirectly because you have more or less money available to spend. In other cases your values influence how you allocate your resources.

A final consideration concerning the relationship of location to life style is *degree of permanency.* There are families that have lived in the same property or apartment for generations. Some individuals live at home, at the same address, until they marry. There are others who have a need to move around, bringing their family with them, so that a child may be enrolled in half a dozen schools or more before he graduates.

Now let us consider one of the most important factors in anyone's life, particularly emphasizing the impact on interpersonal relationships. I am referring to *values.* This may be defined as the worth ascribed to a class of ideas. What I will emphasize are the values attributed to classes of *ideas* which have been influential in human affairs. These ideas *help to organize* one's life style because they have deep feelings associated with them. Strong feelings lead to actions, selection of companions, the guidance offered to children, and other vital choices.

The particular list offered here is based on observation of what it is that many people take seriously. If you grasp the idea that your sense of values is based on deep feelings, often irrational or not put to the test of experience, then you will be well on the road away from self-destructiveness toward emotional common sense. Since this irrational effect of values frequently can be seen in the people around you, the lesson is obvious. One must associate with persons who share one's values or with whom one can come to amicable compromises or learn to accept differences. The alternative to these choices is simply to enter into needless and irrational conflicts and separations from people who otherwise may be very worthy and capable of entering into cordial, mutually worthwhile relationships.

By understanding and developing your values, you will enhance the effectiveness of your decision-making in employment, marriage, selecting friends, and many other areas. Need, drives, values, and goals can be integrated with each other which will result in increased emotional satisfaction and a more productive life. You probably have a number of significant values which vary in importance and may change at different times.

1. *Career/Achievement*. For some people, their professional position is the most important factor in their lives. Their decisions are based on whether their productivity or position will benefit. They sacrifice family, friends, relaxation, etc., in order to concentrate their efforts on professional education, status, and the requirements of a particular position.

2. *People*. To some, the opportunity of relating to individuals or groups of people is the highest value. They enter into careers, clubs, organizations, gatherings, because they get their highest enjoyment from social contact.

3. *Altruism*. This differs from the value of being with people, insofar as the person wants to do things for others rather than being with them. As a result, significant sacrifices are made of one's own welfare so that others may be served. Some professional people and members of religious organizations spring to mind.

4. *Politics*. Affiliations with particular parties or causes is a central factor in the lives of many people. Sometimes identification with particular causes may occur for generations.

5. *Religion*. This value may be central in the life of more people than any other. It is strong enough to provoke wars, schisms between vast numbers of individuals, discord in households, and, in general, vast amounts of hostility. Conversely, deeply held religious values have given individuals strength to stand off the greatest dangers and tribulations. The point made here is the absolute necessity of obtaining an understanding of religious values before entering into intimate relations with others. Then one can be guided by the possible effect of differences.

6. *Materialism*. To many individuals the dollar is God Almighty. Their professional and social decisions are determined by how to get it, who has it, and what happens when you spend it. Materialism means to different people status, security, affirmation of personal worth. Holding materialistic values can also lead a family down the road to debt, tension, crime, bankruptcy, and divorce

when the family income cannot support the economic values.

7. *Culture and aesthetics.* By this I mean devotion to the various arts—painting, music, photography, etc. Shared interests in cultural matters can make a couple's life more intimate and lend scope and direction to activities and social contacts outside the home. But when the wife is into Monteverdi and the husband's chief joy is waking her at 4:00 A.M. to make his breakfast so he can go fishing, and then he brings home fourteen pounds of catch to clean and give to his friends . . .

8. *Learning.* Throughout history there have been men and women whose chief love has been knowledge and philosophy. Those abstractions lead us away from the cares of daily living into what are hoped to be eternal values, or toward concepts which lend deeper understanding and unity to the myriad of objects, creatures, and natural events around us. This value has an honorable past, but it mixes poorly with some others, so watch out.

9. *Family.* To some people family is all. The unity and well-being of their family, including the extended family of cousins, in-laws, etc., is the most important value. All decisions, including marriage, job, location of home, and so forth, are made according to the nearness to and the effect on the family and its sense of value. Unfortunately, taken to an extreme, placing family above all other considerations stifles individuality. It is a direct demand for emotional dependency.

10. *Prestige/Recognition.* Gaining recognition, fame, and honor is a potent value for many individuals. To them, the acclaim of the multitudes, whether it be as a scientist, humanitarian, military leader, artist, etc., is a tremendous driving force. They wish to be able to satisfy themselves that they are important. Probably this is derived from early feelings of inadequacy, so that the real audience for prestige is the unconscious fantasies and memories of childhood figures who were downgrading and unaccepting. Currently unaccepting individuals, such as a spouse, children, friends, or employer, can also act as a spur toward gaining prestige.

11. *Power.* The value placed on power is different from that

placed on prestige. The idea of having influence, telling people what to do, determining events is important to some. In many instances, power is achieved without fame—i.e., the importance of the person pulling the strings of the lives of many others is not known to those who are affected. Indeed, it might be counterproductive if this person's influence was known. The value placed on power over impersonal masses of people is also derived from early feelings of inferiority. The parental figures, and others who created it, may be long since gone, but the wish to be on top remains.

12. *Social utility.* The person who has this value insists that his employment, hobbies, and similar activities must have some kind of importance in the world. His endeavors must be important, and not meaningless, repetitive, of no apparent consequence, or unappreciated. Other individuals, in contrast, feel that they can take any kind of position because they are working for money. They seek their values and enjoyment away from the job, which is merely seen as earning them a living. Social utility differs from altruism because there is no specific intention of being charitable, or of rendering services directly to people, although these are not excluded.

13. *Excitement/Adventure:* People with this value seek a feeling that sends chills of joy down some backs and a *frisson* of terror down others'. The hope for something highly stimulating, perhaps dangerous, thrilling or unexplored, is a romantic vision inspiring them toward exciting experiences and jobs. For them, life without adventure, excitement, or tension of some kind is not worthwhile. Such people skin-dive, sky-dive, climb mountains, join the armed forces, etc. If they are of a more sedentary disposition, they may perform research in the unknown frontiers of knowledge. To other individuals, excitement and adventure are frightening because they threaten their security. They struggle toward a life style in which there is security, probably because heightened sensations of excitement represent to them a form of anxiety.

14. *Variety:* This value has some points in common with *Ex-*

citement/Adventure, but differs because the emphasis is on change rather than on tension. Such people change jobs, living locations, and friends frequently. They have been known to trade in one mate for another before the wedding gifts are unpacked. Employment which involves repetitive tasks is undesirable, while that which creates new experiences is preferable—for example, through traveling, problem-solving, trouble-shooting, meeting different people, and performing new tasks. They go to different restaurants, do not travel twice to the same locale, and enjoy changing furniture and automobiles frequently in their need to avoid boredom.

Having clarified, we hope, many issues which are important in human relationships, we can now start to offer some techniques that will help you to *understand the other person.* Let us repeat our thesis: You have enough intelligence to avoid much of the self-destructiveness you engage in. The road to emotional common sense stresses understanding *not only your needs but the deeply felt needs of the people you associate with.*

Individuals express their feelings and experience life on many levels. One convenient way of regarding the different aspects of experience and communication is dividing it into verbal, non-verbal, and unconscious:

1. *Verbal.* The use of words to express feelings and ideas is certainly the kind of expression that people take most seriously, both in using them and in understanding others. Words are probably the best way to explain certain ideas—for example, science and geography. They are indispensable in writing laws, contracts, and menus. Nevertheless, the alert reader will have noticed that even in the examples offered, words can be replaced by or supplemented by pictures, diagrams, or symbols. The person who relies completely on words to present his feelings and attitudes comes across as dry, uninteresting, and occasionally insincere or lacking insight.

Nevertheless, even though I will describe other means of "reading" others, I place great emphasis on words. They have a potential clarity and unambiguousness not shared by other means of expression. When I deal with others, professionally or personally, I am a great questioner. If I am not sure, I ask. However, once I have ascertained what I consider to be a clear-cut meaning or commitment, I assume that this is what the other party intends. Therefore, *I recommend that the reader not try to be a mind reader.* Rather, if some message is unclear or devious, ask the person to clarify or to repeat. Do not be ashamed to state that you do not understand. Some individuals deliberately develop a devious or confusing style in order to mislead you. Others have been conditioned to avoid expressing their feelings or attitudes clearly because they have been punished as children for being themselves. If you, today, are going to be yourself, you should expect that others will speak to you clearly and sincerely. If they do not, then you must make yourself aware that this is the case.

2. *Non-verbal.* Our identity is established in the eyes of others through our *manner or style* as well as the content of our communications. For some people, style is all. Others prefer an unadorned simplicity. How do others make a non-verbal impression on us?

One thinks immediately of body build: height (from short to tall), weight (emaciated to obese), and breadth (slender to stocky). One also must consider vigor and strength. Considerable information is conveyed by a statement that a man is very tall, undernourished, slender, but seemingly very active and strong. A woman might be described as of average height, overweight, broadly built, inactive, or flabby. There might be seeming contradictions which tell a story—the obese person who remains strong and active, the slender person who has let his muscles deteriorate.

Physical appearance also tells a story. We observe complexion, aesthetic impression, and whether there are any disabilities. Racial identification, a clear or pock-marked skin, degrees of sunburn or pallor are information provided by the complexion. The conformity between cultural stereotypes of beauty and the actual "looks" of a man or woman will affect how they are received socially and on the job market. There is a vast difference in the appearance between many women who can be seen on Seventh Avenue in New York City (the garment and manufacturing district) and Madison Avenue (advertising and other white-collar activities).

We will start our consideration of non-verbal behavior (as opposed to appearance) with the suggestion that it is very helpful to *copy the mannerisms and voice* of the person you are relating with to help you empathize with his attitudes and feelings.

Facial expression provides an important way of reading nonverbal behavior. We look for the smile, the downcast eyes, the worry lines on forehead and cheeks. Some individuals have faces that are always working or twitching; others show no signs of feeling. It is always noteworthy when a mature person has a seemingly carefree, unlined face. Often such a one is not concerned about others. Be suspicious of the fixed smile; it suggests insincerity or a compulsive need to please. The good friend will detect the discrepancy between the appearance of worry and the cheerful verbal message. Is the other party always alert? Perhaps he is suspicious or looking for an opportunity to put into effect the "brass rule" (do unto others before they do unto you). Look into the person's eyes. Do they contact yours or evade them? Self-confidence and honesty show themselves in the glance, but people can train themselves to deceive others.

The voice, the means of vocal expression, offers information apart from the message. Be attentive to enunciation and grammar. By these you can detect the thoughtful, carefully educated person as opposed to the pretentious or pedantic individual who is trying to make an impression. An uneducated person may speak simply and to the point. What I am referring to particularly is the manner of speech. Become alert to slight hesitations which indicate holding back, a flat, unexpressive tone, or sadness, which point to emotional pain or depression. The high-pitched whine indicates a defensive person who always expects opposition and doesn't feel assertive enough to express his needs forcefully. Other people have an insinuating, false quality designed to be seductive and influence you in ways which are not in your best interest. There is a harsh, threatening quality, easily detected, in the person who is looking for the opportunity to be brutal.

Handshake. There is a great deal to be learned from a person's handshake. I recently shook hands with a man whom I met on the street. He had been part of a group that I had evaluated as treating me insincerely and deviously. As I reached toward his hand, he partially withdrew his as though there were slime on mine. All this was supposed to be concealed by his usual big, congealed smile. Did he take me in? No. The directness of the handshake, its flabbiness or artificial forcefulness will reveal much about the underlying intentions of the person in the relationship. It will also be useful to find out if the person is anxious—e.g., whether his hands are cold or sweaty. Since circulatory disorders might contribute to these conditions, if in doubt, ask! You might reveal yourself as a concerned person by determining if a person is nervous or has some medical condition. Perhaps you will save yourself some heartache since the other party may have a good reason to be nervous if he is planning something which you will suffer from!

Posture. Observe how a person carries himself. There is a difference between the erect bearing of the career officer or non-com and the calculated slouch of the equally dedicated dropout. The depressed or discouraged person will portray a message with the shoulders drawn together and the back hunched forward. The high head and springy step of the lover offers a different feeling. The potbelly, lacking any tone, of the elderly or lazy person bespeaks a lack of value placed upon health and vigor. At one time it was considered a measure of one's worldly success to be fat. Today, flabbiness points to giving up the values of health and beauty. Such a person may have some values, but self-esteem is lacking. The wariness of some, the indifference of others, the tension of many are all revealed in posture.

3. *The unconscious level of expression* has been left till last for good reason. It is difficult to understand, though it affects many aspects of behavior. Therefore, I want to give you some awareness

of the general complexity of people's reactions before exposing you to the most perplexing hidden factor of all. By the unconscious is meant a way of reacting to life which is concealed from the person. This does not mean that *others* cannot make accurate estimates of the meaning of his words and actions, only that they are not clear to the actor himself. Ideas, feelings, and action-tendencies often become unconscious because of anxiety. Unconscious meanings come from the childhood experience of disapproval by parents and others. Such feelings as sexual desire, anger, and dependency may not be permitted or might result in punishment. However, emotionally brutalizing parents cannot destroy basic human nature. They can only cause us to hide our real needs. Thus, a person may deny being *hostile* occasionally, but his posture, the way he treats his family and subordinates, an occasional slip of the tongue may indicate a history of anger directed at himself which he is now displacing to others. Similarly with sex. A woman might claim that she has *no sexual desire*, or that her husband completely satisfies her. Closer examination might show seductive postures, provocative reading matter, revealing clothing, and an excessive interest in the sexual development of her children. A person can be taught to rely only on himself and that others are not giving and warm. Thus he may be trained not to show his *dependency*. The relationships he forms would be shown to be very close, demanding, filled with frustration and anger because what is expected is excessive, and the idea of being self-assertive would be frightening to him. Anything that would jeopardize the source of supplies of dependency must be avoided!

Let me warn you, however. Do not be an amateur psychologist! It is far better to insist that people treat you with dignity, respecting your own needs (maybe even unconscious ones), than to try to analyze the unconscious of the next person. Even the pros can make mistakes.

We are ready to point out some of the sources of stress and the effects that they have on you. Then we can learn actively to avoid these tendencies toward self-destructiveness.

6   *Recognizing Stress*

We now have sufficient information to become aware of some destructive forces which can overwhelm us and cause us to be too preoccupied to fulfill our goals and meet our responsibilities. In this chapter I will point out some common kinds of stressful situations and then some of the signs of emotional discomfort which will alert you to take action to protect yourself and improve your situation.

Stress can be defined as a very difficult circumstance or dangerous event, sometimes momentary and sometimes lasting for a long period, which is difficult for a person to cope with. Putting it another way, stress is a change in the individual's world to which he is unable to adjust satisfactorily with his preferred means of adaptation. Under mild stress there may be one of a number of signs of emotional or bodily discomfort. Under prolonged or intense stress there is disorganization of either physiological or emotional functioning, or both.

Stress can result from many causes—e.g., from long term *frustration of basic needs*, from *inability to express basic drives*, *from damage to one's self-esteem*, from *fright or threat of damage of various kinds from the world*, or from *the need to perform beyond one's capacities over an extended period of time*. The earliest signs of stress are the various painful feelings that I will describe later on. The later signs of stress may be psychosis, serious psychosomatic illness, or persistent anxiety or depression which keeps a person from responding adequately to job, friends, and family. Stress may be a direct reaction to *existing events,* a reaction to the *anticipation of forthcoming occurrences,* or a persistent symptom long *after a prior traumatic experience.*

It is self-destructive not to protect yourself, and the first step is to be able to recognize danger. According to Chinese sages, of the thirty-six ways of averting disaster, running away is the best! Certainly not all of the forms of stress can be avoided. It is my hope that you will be able to acknowledge that parts of your life are stressful and then make constructive changes. Perhaps seeing in print the statement that particular events are often destructive to people will enable you to give up any false sense of courage. In other instances, you may perhaps receive some solace from the fact that the painful events of your life have occurred to numerous other people, and the difficulties and discomforts that you experienced are universal events. You will also have a deeper understanding and compassion for the people around you.

Let us now review some of the common stressful circumstances of daily living.

1. *Separation.* This can be caused by the death of a loved person, or the breakup or anticipated breakup of a love relationship or marriage, long separation due to the need to travel, military service, and so forth. A child's separation from his parents due to the death of one of them, or temporary hospitalization, or being repeatedly shifted from one home to another, or the divorce of his parents, is one of the most painful and frequently long-lasting stresses. Some unfortunate individuals often feel a sense of longing and deprivation which keeps them from relating normally to their spouses or others who love them. A great sense of deprivation is experienced, so that the expression of love from others is insufficient to satisfy them. Others experience divorce or the breakup of a love relationship as so painful that it must be averted at all costs

for if it does occur, it may result in depression and anxiety for a long period. An extreme form of separation is the death of a loved person. Some individuals make an adjustment on the basis of an exceptionally close or dependent relationship on a spouse, parent, or child. With the latter's death, they are inadequate to cope with the world, since an excessive amount of support and guidance had been received from the deceased person.

2. *Economic difficulties.* Achieving material necessities is often as complex a factor in a person's life as any of the other areas we ordinarily consider emotional. During the Depression many a family considered itself lucky if there was a single breadwinner earning twenty dollars a week. Today, with inflation, almost thirty-five years of continuous warfare or preparation for it, demands for a higher standard of living, and so forth, even two breadwinners or working people may not be sufficient to keep a family out of debt. Particularly stressful can be the requirement to earn a living while studying, or educating one or more children in private schools or colleges, because of fear of hoodlums, or added transportation expenses due to moving away from the central city with its employment, entertainment, and so forth. However, a further unnecessary cause of stress is "living high off the hog," beyond your means, to the point that your very frame of mind, your basic decisions and your clinging to undesirable employment are a result of economic fear. Medical and legal necessities can also easily wipe out savings and plunge a family into debt.

3. *Fatigue.* The most unappreciated form of stress is fatigue. We all assume that we get tired, but we should also be aware that fatigue can precipitate a psychosis, aggravate medical conditions, create serious automobile and industrial accidents, interfere with personal relationships, and generally result in poor decision-making. It is urgent that when you find yourself in a constant state of fatigue you re-evaluate your life style and make suitable changes. A medical examination might also be indicated. Among the most common causes of fatigue are excessive strains of employment (two jobs, overtime); insufficient help in the household or other

heavy domestic responsibilities; a position that is too physically or mentally exhausting even though it is of normal duration; concurrent study and employment; and excessive travel time to your job. Except in the very young, dissipation is also a cause of fatigue, and sometimes it appears that the price is not worth it. A recent *Time* article (June 5, 1972) pointed out how many kinds of headaches are brought on by stress.

4. *Loss of self-esteem.* Many people, probably including yourself, are trained to depend on other people for praise. While I do not recommend total indifference to the opinions of others, it is still a fact that one cannot control the amount of recognition, praise, or reward which is forthcoming. Thus, it is easy to fall into the trap of overexertion accompanied by aggravation when one's employer, teacher, spouse, or lover is not forthcoming with the kind of eulogies to which you think you are entitled. It must be recognized that many emotionally incompetent individuals hold positions of power, people who are unable to be positive and warm to those who are reliant on them. Thus, if recognition is important to you, you must first obtain an objective evaluation of your performance. Then, if you believe that you are unjustly treated, you should consider making a move, or accept the situation philosophically in return for other advantages, or remain there due to circumstances beyond your control. Particular events which often create a blow to self-esteem include losing a job, unfair criticism, and not receiving an expected prize or praise. More avoidable losses of self-esteem come from falling behind professionally because standards of performance have been raised or one's training is out of date. Here the necessity for hustling is obvious. Further, when age causes an individual to be denied employment or advancement unfairly, it is certainly a blow to one's ego. At this point we will mention a cure we will often refer to: It is vital that you *not rely on a single activity to provide satisfaction in your life.*

5. *Illness.* This condition can affect a large number of other factors in your life. It contributes to fatigue, inability to function economically or provide for the emotional support of one's family,

and the possible loss of valued friends and activities. Illness is a stress which is frequently handled with poor emotional common sense. I know a woman who refuses to go to a physician because "I spent too much time with doctors when I was young." Others neglect serious illness until it proves fatal or conditions develop beyond the point where they can be treated. Illness also creates a stress on the individuals around the sick person, so that it is a matter of simple self-preservation to be interested in the health of all of those whom we care for or are dependent on.

6. *Life style inconsistent with temperament.* This is a somewhat subtle point but can be frequently observed. Consider the shy person who by economic necessity or a foolish attempt to prove himself as self-assertive assumes a position as a salesman. Perhaps an active, muscular, extroverted man is induced by parental pressure to go into a prestigious white-collar position when he might be more suited to be a construction engineer or a forester. Consider a lively, extroverted girl who enjoys social contacts married to a studious, quiet man with a desire for a large family and for confining his social activities to his home. It can be inferred that a person's temperament and personality create an optimal way of relating with people and of solving problems. A person who attempts to live in a manner beyond his strength, intellect, and capacity to respond emotionally is likely to collapse or become disorganized due to stress. We would also like to emphasize that key decisions ought to take into consideration your basic needs, preferred drives, and the way you like to get your kicks (assuming emotional common sense). Otherwise, *the discrepancy between the real you and the world's requirements* will be a source of stress.

7. *Trauma.* This is one of the chief ways in which our defective brain betrays us. Frightening circumstances often haunt us for days, months, and years after they ought to be forgotten. Experiences of being in an accident or near accident, being mugged, assaulted, raped may be so damaging to the ego, may so overload the nervous system, that the memories obsess us. Some individuals radically change their style of life after a traumatic experience to

avoid its recurrence. Others continue their usual activities but are rendered distraught and anxious. When traumatic experiences occur to children, without immediate psychotherapeutic intervention, there may be continued anxiety attacks. Even worse, the experience is "forgotten" only to shape behavior, feelings, and attitudes in a subtle way through the unconscious. Since the continuing effect of trauma may be due to its hidden symbolic meaning—as, for example, a sense of guilt at having contributed to or enjoyed the traumatic experience—psychotherapy is often helpful, causing the individual to understand and then detach from the frightening events. At the least, support from the therapist can help the person to face life with more courage.

8. *Continued conflicts.* It is amazing how some individuals stay in situations that are continuously stressful, relating to unaccepting, combative persons, and in other ways permitting their lives to be made miserable. It is quite stressful to engage in continuous arguments, to struggle to achieve tasks that are too difficult, to prove oneself to someone who is indifferent or listening to different vibes, to hang on to a position which is unsuited to a person's skills, time, resources, and so forth. The wear and tear on the spirit leads to illness, fatigue, emotional discomfort, irritability and other signs of stress which interfere with making correct decisions. From this point on, the road accelerates downhill to disaster. Emotional common sense requires that when you are in a situation of continued conflicts you reconsider whether there may not be a more rewarding alternative.

Having outlined some of the frequent external sources of stress, it is vital that you recognize some of the emotional signs. What I will list here are *forms of emotional discomfort.* They are *signals to you* that you or those you love and value *are in trouble,* are assailed by stress and not adapting properly. They may be the result of self-destructive behavior. They may perhaps be unavoidable effects of realistic events beyond your control. In most cases they are your body's communiqués to you that your ego is being damaged or destroyed and you must take some action on your own behalf.

Similarly, observing these signs of emotional discomfort in your spouse, lover, children, subordinates, employer, teachers, friends should also be a signal that you may have to take action. Any of these people might need your support in a period of crisis. Perhaps in your usual self-destructive way you have provoked feelings which were either unintended or will in some way jeopardize your relationship. Only a self-destructive person lacking emotional common sense will refuse to take action when he observes any of the signs of emotional discomfort in himself or an important person around him.

1. *Anxiety.* This is one of the most disabling of all emotional discomforts and is experienced as a belief in an impending danger that cannot be warded off. One of the characteristics of anxiety is that the nature of the danger is generally vague. It may be due to a symbolic threat or a reminiscence of a prior expectation of punishment or to stimulation by a forbidden impulse such as sex or anger. Many neurotic symptoms evolve in an effort to keep us from experiencing anxiety or because of childish conditioning against expressing our drives.

2. *Guilt feelings.* These are usually neurotic beliefs that one has violated a moral principle and are accompanied by lowered self-esteem. The feeling of having sinned results from a conflict between our conscience, or what we are trained to believe, and our inner drives. The exaggerated feeling of guilt can result in depression and hopeless feelings of devaluation.

3. *Tension.* This is a state of discomfort due either to an uncomfortable situation, as the need to relieve oneself, or to the frustration caused by the inability to express a strong impulse, such as sex or anger. Taken to an extreme, it results in the feeling that one is "about to explode." States of tension interfere with concentration and ultimately can result in a variety of psychosomatic ailments.

4. *Anger or rage.* These feelings and impulses are built into the nervous system as our heritage from the time when we had to

defend ourselves with our bare hands to ensure survival. In children, anger or rage is a typical response to parental authority and is used to say "I won't" in opposition. In adults, it is generally experienced *after* prior feelings of emotional hurt or humiliation. Expressing anger appropriately is one of the most common emotional problems. Many individuals are trained to ignore their feelings or to strike out in an exaggerated way. Still others displace their anger against targets that are totally inappropriate.

5. *Humiliation/Hurt feelings.* The devaluation of our person or of something that we identify with generally is experienced as emotional pain or humiliation. Very often people have specific vulnerabilities or sensitivities because of criticism of parts of their personality—race, religion, etc.—when they were young. Recognition of and response to hurt feelings are often discouraged by guilt-provoking parents (see Chapter 7).

6. *Deprivation.* Not having the luck to be born into a loving, warm, intact family often creates feelings of emptiness and loss which can be carried into adulthood. Then, even with normally responsive mates and friends, a person's need for love may be relatively insatiable. As a result, the capacity for enjoyment is minimal, and unreasonable demands are made on those with whom one comes in contact. This may be the real emotional basis for emotional "clutching."

7. *Depression.* Certainly this is one of the unhappiest feelings, leading in its extreme state to suicide or total withdrawal. Depression is a form of extreme unhappiness, often combined with an inability to be active. It is the result of such stresses as the loss of a loved person through death, the end of a relationship, inability to express anger outwardly, or lowered self-esteem after humiliation.

8. *Rejection.* This is the specific feeling when we are criticized by or forced to retreat from a valued person or group. Some individuals are particularly vulnerable to feelings of rejection and as a result live lives of relative isolation. They do not dare to approach others since they expect rejection. This is likely to be

associated with *chronic low self-esteem*. Thus there is a cycle between an unhappy identity, inability to obtain more positive experiences, and exaggerated fears.

9. *Bad dreams, nightmares, unpleasant fantasies*. These are generally signs of anxiety, traumatic experiences, and continued, unresolved conflicts. Recovery of good spirits is hampered because of fearfulness, inability to sleep, and a pessimistic attitude about the future.

10. *Apathy*. This absence of feeling is a sign that the stress, whether realistic or emotional, has gone on for a very long time. It is a sign that the person considers his situation hopeless and thus is unwilling or unable to rectify it.

11. *Insomnia*. Inability to sleep is a frequent accompaniment of anxiety and depression. Paradoxically, according to W. Zung in "The Pharmacology of Disordered Sleep," in the latter emotional discomfort there seems to be a higher state of arousal than normal, keeping the person from obtaining the restfulness of sleep.

The careful reader now has a good picture of some of the most frequent signs of stress as well as the situations which provoke them. By being alert to these feelings and to the pertinent situation, you may be in a position to reconstruct your life away from self-destructiveness and toward emotional common sense. The next step is to continue learning about your own personality and that of the people with whom you deal. In this way you may be able to make a social diagnosis in order to detect the people and the situations which either elevate your spirits or contribute to your depression.

7 Some Techniques of Practical Self-Understanding

It is interesting to show the practical importance of self-understanding through the comments of Albert Einstein when he was offered what to him must have been the highest honor, the presidency of the State of Israel.

"I am deeply moved by the offer from our State of Israel, and at once saddened and ashamed that I cannot accept it. All my life I have dealt with objective matters, hence I lack both the natural aptitude and the experience to deal properly with people and to exercise official functions. For these reasons alone I should be unsuited to fulfill the duties of that high office, even if advancing age was not making inroads on my strength. . . . I know a little about nature and hardly anything about men."

Can the reader imagine any area of life in which self-understanding cannot help in selecting important, attainable, realistic goals and in which lack of self-understanding can serve as a trap, an enticement toward false dreams of glory and love, an invitation to disaster?

Let me offer a few examples of how lack of self-understanding causes serious problems of living:

1. Mrs. A. had a severe inferiority complex—i.e., she did not realize her true worth and personality. Her lack of confidence in

making correct decisions permitted her to accept an offer from an inappropriate man and a subsequent bad marriage.

2. Young B. was unaware of his inability to get along with people. Thus, he permitted himself to select college training in labor relations. As he put it, when he tried to perform his job he discovered "I still couldn't get along with people." This caused him to have vocational difficulties.

3. Miss C. did not realize her need for affection and kept giving signals to men not to be too intimate. On one occasion, with a particularly appropriate date, she was cold to him, not recognizing his feelings until later when his voice cracked. Subsequently she became warmer, stating, "I got shocked into feeling that I had to change."

You will recall from Chapters 4, 5, and 6 that important factors in your personality are your style of adaptation (emphasizing temperament and constitution), your needs, basic drives, sense of personal identity, style of life, and the kind of signals that you send yourself to let you know that stress is beginning to affect you.

I emphasize here the importance of understanding your feelings, which includes the realization that they can mislead you. Yes, I said that your feelings can mislead you. Certainly there are people who have told you to "trust your feelings." Believe me, they are misguided, and if you are to avoid self-destructiveness you must tell them so and learn the reality about your feelings.

To really understand your feelings, you must be able to label them correctly and to identify the situation (past, present, or anticipated) which stirred them up. When you have become aware that you are experiencing something important, you must try to identify the kind of feeling it is. The next task is to check it out—that is, to determine whether your feelings are *appropriate*. Only then can you be certain that acting according to your feelings will enhance your well-being and not be self-destructive.

You may wish to ask, Isn't this a complex process? Isn't one of the criteria of happy living a feeling of spontaneity? Of course, a carefree spontaneity is a blessing, a state of mind enjoyed rarely by many people. What seems to be the case more often is that people are driven to action by unpleasant feelings—for example, anger, anxiety, guilt, and so many of the other symptoms of emotional distress discussed in Chapter 6. However, as certainly as the sun will rise tomorrow, most of these feelings are related to the inculcation of childish values, unconscious symbolic reactions adding false meanings to events and people, inaccurately low estimates of self-esteem, childhood punishments unrelated to the present, and so forth. Therefore, if you trust your feelings as giving you reliable information about what is going on around you without checking them out frequently, you will have the effectiveness and reality-testing of a navigator using astronomical charts about twenty years old.

It is certain that as you consider the relationship between your feelings and the people and events which affect you you will begin to see that in many cases there is a significant mismatch. You will discover that the feeling of anxiety or low self-esteem is unfounded. Many of the people with whom you experience these are well intentioned toward you and accepting of you. Perhaps you will also discover that your little humorous stunt of teasing your children or your secretary is accompanied by malevolence—the enjoyment of somebody else's pain. Perhaps that feeling of anger is not caused by the person you have just chewed out but is displaced from work, or really based on a misunderstanding. It is likely that as you check out your feelings and then take courses of action which use emotional common sense, you will experience more rewards, successes, friendships and fewer rejections and failures. Why? Because you will be emotionally appropriate and really in touch simultaneously with your feelings and those of the important people around you.

Closely allied to understanding your feelings is acknowledging your basic needs (for love, security and dependency, sex, status, and companionship). People grow up with differing deficits to be supplied by the world but also with different degrees of understanding and acceptance of these needs. At one time it was believed even in some educated quarters that females had no sexual needs. While this seems to be ridiculously inadequate thinking today, it was so widely accepted by both men and women that an entire school of psychotherapy (i.e., psychoanalysis), indeed the whole modern history of dynamic personality theory, could begin with the understanding and amelioration of sexual anxiety.

Today, according to my experience, the *need which is least understood is dependency.* Both sexes, although primarily men, are taught to be self-reliant. When the creed that "it is better to give than to receive" was added to the emphasis on maturity and responsibility, then a whole generation of people was trained to think that to give is noble, to accept is rotten, and spiritual interdependence of humanity is a fiction. It is also true that a couple of generations of "momism" (cf. Philip Wylie's *Generation of Vipers*) and other forms of control through "giving" have also made it unpalatable to accept graciously the offerings of others. In extreme situations individuals become depleted and incapable of functioning under continued stress when they cannot accept their emotional dependency on others.

It should be recognized, moreover, that needs change. The particular needs of childhood or adolescence are not identical with those of maturity or old age. The need for acceptance, love, and vindication becomes attached to images and fantasies in early years. These special combinations of images, feelings, and particular trends toward action are retained and influence us in later years. We become particular kinds of lovers, parents, employers, etc., to act out the idealized figures or vengeful fantasies of youth. When we propel these action trends into reality, we then discover that we need different responses from people than we obtain and are regarded by others as inappropriate, intrusive, or generally "sickies." (See R.S. Parker's "Anger, Identification, and Irrational Target Selection.")

The feeling that is most expressed today is hostility. The amount of destructiveness that is expressed and justified these days is extraordinary. Even peaceful conditions are hated by some—but let us hold that until Chapter 11 on anger.

To make you more aware of some of the important characteristics of your daily functioning, as well as to make your perceptions of the social world around you much sharper, I am providing you with two self-administered check lists and a social-feelings questionnaire. Please understand that there are no right or wrong answers. Furthermore, I will not mislead you by suggesting the meaning of any hypothetical scores. The only purpose of these is to improve your self- and social understanding.

I suggest that you start with the check list "Significant Traits in Which People Differ." Evaluate yourself on the different traits. Then evaluate one or two people with whom you have an important relationship. Finally, try to figure out how the similarities and differences between you add strength or conflict to the relationship. The source of this list is partially the writer's own experience and partially J. P. Guilford's *Personality* and R. B. Cattell's *The Scientific Analysis of Personality.*

Then you may refer to the "Emotional Problem Area Check List." This is based on the many emotional problems my patients have expressed to me over the years. You may discover that certain general areas are particularly troublesome to you. You may also discover that your thinking has become clearer as a result of having some emotional problems described in print.

Finally, you will study the "Social Relationship Self-Interview." This will be particularly valuable in choosing a mate or discovering the sources of stress in married life.

SIGNIFICANT TRAITS IN WHICH PEOPLE DIFFER

Name			
Social Role	Self-assertion, domination, leader	versus	Timidity, submissiveness, compliance, follower
Trust	Trusting, friendly, poised, self-confident, secure	versus	Self-conscious, insecure, hostile, suspicious, inferiority feelings
Sociability	Outgoing, spontaneous, warmhearted	versus	Shy, inhibited, self-sufficient, aloof
Vigilance	Alert	versus	Inattentive
Personality	Extroverted (interested in others)	versus	Introverted (interested in one's own imagination)
Reality			
Attitude	Carefree, happy-go-lucky	versus	Sober, deliberate, serious, self-controlled
Toughness	Tender-minded, sentimental	versus	Tough-minded, realistic
Mood Quality	Cheerful	versus	Depressed
Acceptance			
of Others	Tolerant	versus	Critical
Sexual			
Identification	Masculine	versus	Feminine
Mood Stability	Stable	versus	Cyclical mood swings
Mental Stability	Composed, good adjustment	versus	Nervous, anxious, self-conscious
Development	Mature, controlled	versus	Immature, childish, acting-out, impulsive
Authority	Conformity or non-conformity	versus	Independence

EMOTIONAL PROBLEM AREA CHECK LIST

I. FAMILY: I have difficulty in my relationship(s) with:
a. Father   e. Brother
b. Mother   f. Sister
c. My child or   g. In-law
    children   h. Other family member
d. Husband or wife

II. EMOTIONAL LIFE: I show the following signs of stress:
a. General anxiety or nervousness   i. I suffered from rejection as a child
b. Fears of____   j. I have always had low self-esteem
c. Guilt feelings about____   k. I have nightmares, unpleasant daydreams
d. I get tense when____   l. I feel apathetic
e. I get angry when____   m. I can't sleep properly
f. I get humiliated when____   n. Stress causes these bodily symptoms____

g. I feel depressed
h. I suffer from rejection now

III. FEELINGS ABOUT LIFE OR MY IDENTITY:
a. I am considered domineering
b. I am indecisive
c. I am too passive
d. I lack self-esteem/sense of value
e. I was taught false expectations from life
f. I can't act according to my ethics/morals
g. I am repelled by society
h. People don't give me the respect I deserve
i. I had poor guidance or models from parents
j. My values/goals/beliefs are unclear

IV. SEXUAL PROBLEMS:
a. I am inexperienced or lack knowledge
b. I am shy
c. I cannot express love
d. I antagonize through manipulating
e. I feel easily manipulated
f. I feel unattractive
g. I have little sex drive
h. I feel excessive sexual drive
i. I think sex is dirty
j. I am too idealistic
k. Sex is unsatisfying/can't achieve orgasm
l. Sex makes me feel guilty

m. I can't find a partner who shares my values
n. Confidential____

V. SOCIAL RELATIONS:
a. I fight excessively with authority
b. I can't get close to people
c. I take on too many obligations
d. I am too dependent
e. I am too independent
f. I am naïve or inexperienced
g. My suspiciousness keeps others away
h. Other____

VI. WORK OR SCHOOL:
a. I have difficulty concentrating
b. I lack motivation to continue/to drive onward
c. My skills are insufficient for my job
d. I need specific advice
e. I am fearful of changing jobs
f. I fight with my supervisor
g. I have difficulties with subordinates
h. I am uninterested in work/school
i. I am nervous before authority
j. My goals are unclear
k. I can't achieve my goals
l. I keep losing my job/being dropped from schools
m. I lack skills for advancement
n. I fight with colleagues
o. I work below my real level
p. I can't talk before groups
q. Other____

VII. HEALTH:
a. I have a weight problem
b. I lack stamina/am always tired
c. My impediment hampers me
d. I always feel ill
e. Sleep problem
f. I have trouble with____

VIII. INTELLECTUAL LIFE:
a. I am troubled by certain thoughts
b. I have no interests or hobbies
c. My memory isn't good enough
d. I have trouble learning new things
e. I have difficulty concentrating
f. Other____

IX. AREAS OF STRESS:
   a. Separation
   b. Economic problems
   c. Fatigue
   d. Loss of self-esteem
   e. Illness
   f. Life style inconsistent with temperament
   g. Trauma
   h. Continued conflicts
   i. Other____

THE SOCIAL RELATIONSHIP SELF-INTERVIEW

1. How am I being treated?
2. How do I feel?
3. Am I pursuing my goals?
4. Are our life styles consistent?
5. Am I free to feel, act, talk the way I want to?
6. Do I feel respect or criticism for him/her?
7. Am I transferring or displacing from other relationships to this relationship?
8. Do I have other resources?
9. Am I relating to this person because loneliness is terrible?
10. When I am angry, do we resolve our problems, ignore them, or make them worse?
11. Do I live for my needs, the other person's needs, or both?
12. How does he treat others?
13. Is he consistent in what he says and does?
14. Is he truthful or lying?
15. Does he express his feelings, attitudes, intentions, goals?
16. Is he supportive in time of difficulty?
17. Does he take initiative in proposing activities?

8 Coping with Emotional Pain

I hope that by this time you have made a self-evaluation of your emotional discomforts and of the stresses in your life. If you have, you are now ready to begin the task of reducing self-destructiveness and increasing your emotional common sense.

Emotional pain, humiliation, and vulnerability are the key to many of your most unhappy hours and days. I intend to show you that it is not only urgent that you recognize these feelings in yourself but imperative, indeed justified, that you express them. There is as much damage done to individuals in the area of stifling their hurt feelings as there is in forbidding their sexuality and preventing their self-assertion.

Let us again return to the question of the nature of feelings. To remind you, feelings are a signal that important events are taking place. It is meaningless to ask whether feelings are rational, because rationality implies a different although equally valuable phase of experience. It is more meaningful to ask what are the events that stirred up the feelings, what are the feelings like, have we properly interpreted what is happening to us, what action will be consistent with our welfare and what will be self-destructive?

Emotional pain or humiliation is experienced by people who feel vulnerable or sensitive. While it is possible to describe some

72

people as being excessively sensitive, most people are trained not to show their pain, regardless of its extent. This is the epitome of self-destructiveness since it gives others a hunting license with us as a target. More about this later. The basis for emotional pain is the experience of being treated with disdain when one is a child. The child who is respected by his or her parents, who is not overwhelmed with criticism or punishment, grows up with a sense of values which is not easily disturbed by the large number of destructive people in this world. Often enough the vulnerable person has his self-esteem rendered fragile by parents who themselves were not only victims of inadequacy feelings but who turned around and bullied their children. How often does a parent degrade a child's best efforts? Perhaps this disapproval is indirect —for example, expecting perfection so that even good effort is treated as being inadequate. Another favorite way of manipulating a child is through provoking guilt. I had a fifty-year-old patient who insisted that he would be the death of his still alive eighty-five-year-old mother. Playing favorites of one child over another makes the rejected child feel valueless and angry. Sometimes a child is mercilessly compared to others: Their achievement is so much better than yours. Another route to vulnerability is to be bullied by neighborhood toughs without parental solace or protection.

It is certainly a truism that children are far more emotional than adults. When they are threatened, they object, they cry, they retreat, or ultimately they may withdraw. All these are cues to observant and caring parents that their children's feelings are hurt, that they are overwhelmed by stronger forces, that their growing egos are being misshapen and left with wounds, scars, and defenseless areas. The sensitive parent will then try to make amends or to change. Perhaps to undo the damage the child will be sent to psychotherapy, and the parents will participate in counseling.

More often, however, the parents are motivated to teach the child not to express his pain in order to keep themselves from feeling guilty and sometimes to keep the child as a target to enable themselves to feel superior.

The emphasis I place upon the role of pain inhibition in self-destructive behavior can be observed from the fact that this chapter is the first on coping with specific problem areas. I want you to be able to recognize it in yourself and to avoid inflicting it on your children. After we see some of the symptoms of pain inhibition, I will show you some of the specific ways in which parents teach their children not to annoy them by showing their feelings. Then you will learn how to cope with the emotional pain that you may experience.

I define pain inhibition as the inability to express hurt feelings in social relationships, with the intention of improving the relationship subsequent to the encounter. (Much of the subsequent discussion is based on the article "The Patient Who Cannot Express Pain," by R. S. Parker in the book *The Emotional Stress of War, Violence, and Peace*.) You can recognize that you suffer from pain inhibition if you have some of the following characteristics: diminished sense of self-respect, frequent depressions, feeling of shame, inability to assert yourself, detachment of social anxieties, holding back anger until you are in a rage, inability to express love or to ask for emotional support, and a proneness to feel exploited by others.

If you suffer from these symptoms, you are in serious trouble, and you have not learned how to defend yourself from destructive people. I assert that it is important for you to express your pain and then observe the reaction of those who have offended you. But it is also important that you understand the *relationship between pain and anger*. Some people assert that anger is a primary feeling. When we are attacked in some way we get angry. Obviously, this is a marvelously true statement for a carnivore such as a lion or even for an elasmobranch such as a shark, but it is an inaccurate simplification for a complex mentality such as yours. After all, between the behavior of another person and your response is that conceptual-emotional system which we have called your self-concept. This image conjures up a variety of feelings and symbolic meanings when activity from the world is relevant to it. Sometimes it is involved even when no activity is really related to it. If you perceive the actions of another as damaging to your self-esteem or best interests, then you are likely first to experience emotional pain or humiliation. Then, and only then, unless you are a shark, you become angry. Let me repeat: pain precedes anger.

Since by now you are a sophisticated student of human nature, you wisely ask why it is that I (or someone you know) get angry but I am not aware of pain. The reason is simply this: Many households and many influences in our culture discourage the expression of pain (and also of anger). What seems to happen is that, first, the overt observable expression of emotional pain is held back. Then the actual feeling is inhibited. Thus some people may not be aware that unconsciously they feel humiliated, tormented, or abused.

The social relationships of people who do not experience or express their pain have definite self-destructive characteristics. It must be remembered that neither pain nor anger go away. They build up and may be expressed suddenly, excessively, and against the wrong target on unpredictable occasions. What often happens is that the pain-inhibiting adult, probably just like yourself, builds up anger and finally, when "the last straw breaks the camel's back," has an outburst of rage and hopelessly ruins a relationship or continues in an overly sensitive, inflamed mood. The relationship where one person inflicts pain and another inhibits it is filled with resentment, with the destructive experience not changing. Sometimes the situation is made even worse by the pain inhibitor's refusal or inability to express his feelings. Since it is sometimes experienced as frustrating when one party does not express his feelings, if the passivity is considered to be an invitation to continue the abuse, this torment is likely to be continued.

At this point it will be useful to study those home influences which encourage the emotional crippling I have described as pain inhibition (Parker, 1972b). If you are now a parent, or plan to be, or perhaps you have responsibilities for children as a teacher or counselor, the discussion will merit considerable attention. I believe that households can be described as being of four kinds: expressive, nice, abusive, and unresponsive.

The *expressive household* is the one in which feelings are encouraged as legitimate and the child's ego is built up because he is treated as a valuable individual.

The *nice household* discourages the expression of strong feelings of pain and anger. They can be communicated only in carefully modulated, disguised ways. What reasons can possibly be given in a respectable household to discourage such basic experiences as humiliation? First, there are very specific ideologies which emphasize strength and discourage weakness. It is more important to express love or charity or to live in a genteel way than to experience and recognize such a basic feeling as pain. An illustration may be found in Chekhov's play *The Three Sisters*. Roger Garris in his *New York Times* review of the play on August 10, 1969, made the point admirably: "It's a play about the consequences of living by a certain code of courtesy, taste, and gentility. . . . The dark under side of the sisters' hypersensitivity about other people's manners is their trained incapacity to recognize other people's violent impulses and intentions."

Sometimes parents tell the child to cover up conflict, impoverishment, scandal, or ethnic background so that they, *the parents*, do not experience shame. The child can be taught that the only way to have self-respect is to conceal pain and weakness. Such precepts are offered as "Don't be a cry baby," "Don't show others your weakness or they will take advantage of you," "Keep a stiff upper lip," and other drivel. A parent can tell a child not to show feelings due to so-called realistic considerations. One of my patients lost her mother when she was five and was required to live with cold, detached relatives. This was probably a result of the father's own emotional inadequacies. As she put it, "I was slapped down for expressing feelings, and my father told me, 'This is the situation and you have to accept it.'"

Sometimes in so-called *nice* homes, guilt-provoking techniques keep the child in line. The child's efforts to assert his independence and individuality are inhibited through predicting dire consequences, such as the death of the parent or the excessive shame or danger brought on by legitimate activities. Among the self-destructive acts of people who were raised by guilt-provoking parents are entering into sado-masochistic relationships (to obtain an unachievable vindication) with hostile, punishing partners who are rejecting and who create further resentment and anger. Such individuals also, in extreme cases, commit crimes ranging from the trivial to the vicious in order to obtain the punishment they believe they deserve and in order to relieve their sense of guilt. I have discussed in detail elsewhere this extreme form of self-destruction, which may require that they commit murder so that the state will execute them.

Let us consider the *abusive home.* In this atmosphere, anger and pain are magnified because of personal experience, or the model of the parents, of physical and/or verbal abuse in response to opposition. To be resentful is to be punished. Frequently, the situation is made worse by *poor parental models.* One parent may be attacked by the other and not further the conflict for some reason. If the child identifies with the passive victim, he becomes self-destructive, since he may be incapacitated by a feeling of helplessness before aggressors, accompanied by contempt for the victim (his parent or others), and ultimately by a feeling of detachment. As an adult, when he is attacked, his defenses are hampered, and finally he experiences waves of destructive anger or crippling fear.

When the child is personally attacked by a cruel parent, a distorted sense of life results, and there is a distinct likelihood of repeating the parental brutality. The onslaught can be made worse if the child makes a game of resistance by refusing to give satisfaction through expressing pain. One man, beaten into unconsciousness by his father, described his reaction as follows: "No matter how much you hurt me I won't cry."

The final instance of a pain-inhibiting household I describe as *emotionally depriving.* There are some compulsive, inflexible parents who rob a child of his independence and belief that his feelings are valuable through repetitive criticism for deviations from parental instructions and values. These parents do not recognize that their children are maturing and developing different concepts of the world. With them, "It does no good to express hurt feelings; in fact it would make matters worse." These parents refuse to change or to stop dominating their children. Other parents are downright exploitative. They deprive their children of medical attention, violate their desires, or sacrifice one child to another. They infantilize the child to retain him and in many ways use the child for their own ego trips. Finally, there are those unresponsive parents who are incapable of expressing, or choose not to express, their feelings toward their children. To become emotionally involved is to have added responsibilities. Their motto is: "I don't want to hear your troubles." Such a child first experiences personal devaluation and then is self-destructive, since he believes that his feelings have no influence on others. Furthermore, he never learns to evaluate the feelings of others, since his parents did not express feelings to accompany their actions.

After this discussion of how individuals become vulnerable and then cannot defend themselves, we are able to offer some positive steps toward *coping with emotional pain.*

The first step in coping with emotional pain is to recognize it. We have already pointed out some techniques for becoming sensitive to the connection between social events and your feelings. This is a two-way process. As you learn to recognize whether other people are treating you with respect, you will be able to label those feelings which accompany abrasive situations as painful, humiliating, and so on.

The next step is equally vital. I call it *"the ouch principle."* It is so simple that you will be immediately ashamed that you did not discover it yourself. When somebody steps on your toes, say,

"Ouch." It is truly amazing to consider the vast number of people who violate "the ouch principle." I became particularly aware of this when I suggested to one of my therapy groups that people can be divided into those who *elevate* and those who *depress one's spirits.* The look of enlightenment and happiness that they expressed told me that the group members understood this simple description of human interaction as being very valuable.

After you have said "Ouch," or "You have hurt my feelings," or "I don't like the way I am being treated," then it is important that you watch the reaction of the other person. Some people will be genuinely chagrined that they have offended you. They will express their concern. Value them. Others will try to explain why they have acted the way they did. It may be that there was a misunderstanding, that they did not mean to be offensive, or perhaps their criticism was justified and you are genuinely oversensitive. In this case, the relationship can also be maintained through the interchange of honest feelings.

However, there are others whose emotional reactions to being told that they have hurt your feelings will be quite different. They will deny it or accuse you of being overly sensitive. They will maintain that they have a right to their opinions. Perhaps they will try to hurt you again because they have found a weak spot. The only way that you can identify these vicious people is to *take a risk by expressing your feelings.* It ought not to be hard to separate those individuals who are emotionally expressive without intending to downgrade you from those who will continue to do so regardless of how you feel.

The next step is to *eliminate resolutely from your life those people who are indifferent or hurtful to your feelings.* There is nothing in your experience that is more important than your feelings. Generally, almost any kind of hardship can be borne with decent grace if one's self-respect can be maintained. It is self-destructive to associate with so-called friends, abusive employers, mean spouses, abusive offspring if there is any alternative. I repeat: The most satisfactory way of coping with emotional pain is to identify those people who elevate your spirits and eliminate those who depress them. I have done this myself after the most serious crisis of my own life and have never regretted it. It is self-destructive to be gnawed away at in the name of friendship, loyalty, family, and other abstractions. It is emotional common sense to surround yourself with those who value you, who try to make you feel good, who forgive you your faults, who support you when the going is rough.

Since you may be sufficiently self-destructive not to take this emotional common sense at its face value, let me take up some objections which have been made to it. One person accused me of instigating guilt-provoking behavior. If by this is meant a technique of preying on others' weaknesses, I say this is ridiculous. In the first place, many people who provoke hurt feelings are really guilty of emotional or physical brutality. Secondly, such opponents of pain expression believe that one should defend oneself through the immediate, direct expression of anger. This is a particularly destructive point of view. There is already a vast amount of unreasoned anger in the world. By expressing pain early in a relationship, *before serious anger develops,* the individual has a number of options. He can explain his position, inquire into the feelings of the other person, be angry, leave, and so forth. He does not immediately provoke a fight and thus risk *making the situation immediately worse.*

It should be noted that there are ways of protecting oneself which do make the situation worse. Please remember that there is a *difference between saying "You hurt my feelings" and making an accusation.* "I feel humiliated" brings out one response from a person, and "You are a son of a bitch" brings out another. It is generally wiser to express your own feelings first and then later, if the situation warrants, to point out the inadequacies of the other. The latter step, unless tactfully handled, may be experienced as a provocation for a fight or the end of a relationship. Unless you mean either of these, proceed with caution.

What about the question of revealing your vulnerability? It is quite likely that your overly sensitive areas have already been targeted by your opponent, so the risk of further damage to your ego is minimal. The benefits from expressing your hurt are maximal, since you can clearly identify friends from foes. Think of the soldier who raises his helmet on a stick to see if it will be fired on!

One reason that is frequently given for staying in an abusive relationship is the fear of loneliness. "If I don't accept the pain, there is the greater pain of eternal loneliness." We shall discuss this problem of emotional deprivation later, but let me state quite categorically: Get rid of the pain-provoking person, then you will have the time and good spirits to find someone who will value and care for you and stir up warmth and love.

Finally, it is most important that you develop other resources which will occupy your time and enhance your self-esteem.

Will one person's maturity provoke pain in the immature?

Since maturity is related to the adequacy with which we deal with our inadequacies, don't these inadequacies become the stronger motivation in relationships? — In a marriage can't these become an inhibiting force to the partner?

9 *Alleviating Guilt, Anxiety, and Worthlessness*

The painful feelings treated in this chapter are further proof of the harmfulness of the dictum that "You must always trust your feelings." The feelings of being guilty, anxious, and worthless are common, intense, immobilizing, and generally without any reference to reality. It is one of the swiftest throughways on the route to self-destructiveness to make decisions on the basis of being an inferior, wrongdoing person.

I would like to make it clear at the beginning that I am not stating that "anything goes" in human relations, so that no matter what we do to others we ought to be free of guilt. I think that I have made my position quite clear that people are vulnerable, and the aftereffects of bad treatment can be extensive and long-lasting. What is clear, however, is that many people who are basically decent, productive, and considerate of others' feelings travel through life as though they were sinners about to be condemned to one of Dante's circles in the Inferno: "I entered on the roadway deep and wild and saw these words inscribed upon a rock: THROUGH ME LIES THE ROAD TO THE CITY OF GRIEF: THROUGH ME LIES THE PATHWAY TO WOE EVERLASTING: THROUGH ME LIES THE ROAD TO THE SOULS THAT ARE LOST . . . ABANDON HOPE, ALL

YE WHO ENTER HERE!" (Cantos 2, 3, tr. by Lawrence Grant White.)

The determination of the overwhelming role that anxiety plays in the life of many people was one of the significant contributions of Sigmund Freud. (See particularly *Inhibitions, Symptoms, and Anxiety,* sometimes translated as *The Problem of Anxiety.*) He pointed out that anxiety takes many forms and that it is the basis for many of the major mental symptoms. It would be correct to state that many people's lives are organized around the fact that they experience considerable anxiety or guilt, or they must go through extreme efforts and contortions of their world in order to avert it. Freud also laid the groundwork for understanding the connection between anxiety, guilt, and feelings of worthlessness.

It is useful for you to understand the forms and origins of anxiety in order for you to judge whether you ought to overcome it, or whether it is alerting you to a realistic danger in your life. It is self-destructive to assume that because you are nervous, guilty, or feel valueless you are condemned to a life of emotional discomfort and severely restricted activities.

Freud recognized many forms of anxiety, including separation anxiety or fear of loss of the mother (we shall consider this in the chapter on loneliness), danger from the external world (realistic anxiety), from the id (which becomes neurosis), and from the superego (the origin of guilt). At this point I suggest that you glance back at Chapters 2 and 3, wherein I point out that many of our values are developed in childhood, and we have one hell of a time trying to get rid of them. In fact, we aren't even aware that they relate to a time, place, and situation in which we were weak, dependent, and emotionally vulnerable.

Realistic anxiety certainly exists. There are many familiar examples—for example, the aftereffects of a confrontation with a hoodlum on the street, a narrow escape from a reckless driver while in a car, the feeling of a truck careening down on us while crossing a road. This kind of anxiety is usually a correct signal that we are,

anxieties relate to above.

or have been, in danger. Nevertheless, the way people handle realistic anxiety is often irrational. I myself did not learn to drive a car until I was twenty-six because of an excessive fear of being injured or of injuring others. Some people are reluctant to try new activities because they were taught as children that the world is a very fearful place. As a result, travel, meeting new people, venturing into the streets at night, and so on, become excessively troublesome to them. As two people put it, anxiety is "going through customs with three bottles" or even "going through customs with nothing to hide."

Other people take the opposite tack. They violate all common-sense precepts concerning care of their physical well-being. *They court danger.* Many examples come to mind: the girl who hitch-hikes, the chronic speeder, the sky diver, the excessive smoker, and so forth. On close observation these individuals are engaged in self-destruction. Many of them were fearful children and carry the illusion that they have to prove themselves to be adequate. The irrationality of the belief, and the strength with which it is held, is testified to by the extremes to which the disproof is carried. Other individuals carry in their minds some false ideal as to the amount of daring or social revolt that is necessary for them to feel worthwhile. They imagine a crowd cheering them on, booing if they are "chicken," which is the real source of their daring. Their sense of valuelessness causes them to take the extreme position of conjuring up admirers and then performing for this hallucinated cheering section. Still others enter into what would ordinarily be anxiety-provoking situations because they are depressed and hopeless. They really want to die. They do not have the courage to take their life directly, so they hope that their misery will be alleviated through "an accident." Of course, they may end up maimed, or cause death and injury to others as well.

It is emotional common sense to look not only at the consequences of one's actions but also at their origins. I shall make the point repeatedly that self-understanding is a complex task that involves integrating knowledge of one's basic needs and values, one's feelings at a particular time, the personal relationships involved in a situation, and the attempt to function toward the achievement of some vital goal. Thus, to give in to realistic anxiety means to restrict one's friends and activities and to reduce the possibility of achieving something worthwhile in the grand scale of one's life. On the other hand, to be daring or reckless may mean that one is engaged in activities which may have some value, or may only mean performing for some imaginary audience such as a gallery of relatives, neighborhood punks, negativistic teachers who put you down unmercifully.

Neurotic anxiety is usually differentiated from *fear* because it does not seem to be directed toward any particular object. The soldier under fire, the person who thinks that his house is being broken into, the airplane passenger who is caught in sudden turbulence are all too well aware of their fear. Neurotic anxiety, on the other hand, is characterized by its pervasiveness and vagueness. It should be differentiated from a *phobia*, which is an unreasonable fear of a particular object or situation sufficiently intense to hamper a person's life.

How can you recognize if you suffer from neurotic anxiety? One answer is found in H. Laughlin's *The Neuroses:* "Anxiety may be regarded as pathologic when it is present to such an extent as to interfere with: (1) effectiveness in living, (2) the achievement of realistic goals or satisfactions, or (3) reasonable emotional comfort." Anxiety attacks are characterized by their suddenness, with both an emotional part (dread, apprehension, fear, terror) and a physiological reaction (heart palpitations, pain in the chest, fainting, cold hands or flushing, dizziness, numbness, perspiration, and disorders of the gastrointestinal tract, sexual organs, and neuromuscular systems). In fact, there are many serious mental problems which include the symptom of anxiety and a variety of specific medical conditions which either mimic it or bring on various symptoms similar to anxiety.

Emotional common sense, then, demands a vigorous attitude toward alleviating anxiety. First, it must be understood. Second, you must exercise self-discipline to unlearn old habits, and finally, if these do not markedly reduce your discomfort, you should obtain whatever psychotherapeutic or medical assistance is necessary to bring your spirits back to well-being.

It is necessary to understand *anxiety, guilt, worthlessness,* and *phobias* in the light of both experience and heredity. It is likely that some people have a genetic disposition to experience new events with vulnerability, while others have the supreme gift of relative fearlessness. It has been extremely useful to me in my clinical practice to have my patients remember themselves as children or to ask their parents about their level of anxiety at an early age. Even well-meaning, non-neurotic parents can give birth to an anxious child. How they treat the child is another matter. The person who is anxious from birth, shows startled reactions, fear of strangers, etc., may be more likely to attach his feelings to particular kinds of events, such as criticism, punishment, and fear of rejection.

While this reaction trend can be accounted for by psychological theories of learning and reinforcement, many states of anxiety are induced by parental teachings and attitudes. We have not only a self-concept and attitude toward reality (ego), but we also have a set of standards by which we judge ourselves—i.e., morality and a conscience (ego-ideal or superego). Neurotic anxiety is due in part to our estimate that our basic drives (sex and anger particularly) will get us into trouble. This kind of fear is largely the basis for hysterical symptoms, obsessions, compulsions, and other forms of what used to be called abnormal psychology and is now referred to as psychopathology. Only when these *defenses against anxiety* fail or have not developed in the first place do we experience anxiety.

Therefore, your experience of anxiety or the development of embarrassing, uncomfortable, or crippling emotional symptoms is a result of what you have been trained to believe will be the consequences of your actions. If you were told that your father would cut your penis off if you masturbated, you are entitled to sexual anxiety. Perhaps your mother strapped you when she caught you necking with the boy next door. All kinds of mistreatment are inflicted on children and youth for sexual activity. Similarly for anger. It is absolutely natural for children to be angry. Nevertheless, to react with anger may be an invitation to be hit, sent away from the table, screamed at, and deprived. As a result, when new situations arouse feelings of anger, the experience of anxiety arises for fear of the consequences.

Very often the actual situation that arouses anxiety is far removed from the original threat. There may be a recollection of somebody like the punishing parent; there may be a hostile or sexually provocative person who stirs up our feelings. Perhaps there is a locale which reminds us of a deeply experienced sexual or hostile event in which we took part or for which we were punished. The result is the anxiety attack or the formation or increase of some symptoms. The trouble with symptoms is that they frequently represent not only the prevention of the drive and some emotional crippling, but unconsciously they *also provide satisfaction* so that they are likely to be maintained. If one is prone to become anxious, a vague but distressing anxiety attack usually causes all other activities to cease while the individual struggles to regain his composure. The strength of the fear is measured by the fact that anxiety can be misinterpreted as a developing heart attack.

We come now to guilt. Questions of morality are generally related to early training. It is true that some people may have a profound change in their values during maturity, but that is generally under the impact of new, disturbing situations with which the old attitudes could not cope. As part of our maturation we develop some attitude concerning what standards we should accept. Familiar examples are the variety of religious codes, but as if this were not enough there are many family credos which are based on the peculiarities of the idiots who teach them. I had a patient who was taught by his grandfather that "people are either steel to be hammered, or the anvils upon which they are shaped." As a result, he thought that all human relationships involved the sense of power, and he himself felt constantly "shaped" by others and thus powerless.

Moral codes involve, of course, how we should act. But after all, actions are generally directed at particular people or groups of people. Any standard of behavior or moral code, then, has to affect our human relationships. We may have been shaped by eternal fire and brimstone, by fear of rejection or isolation, by condemnation, or by public scorn. In addition to the fear of what people will say about us and the consequences of a little passion or anger *(guilt)*, we can also develop a sense that our entire person is valueless *(low self-esteem)*. We learn that what we have done condemns us as entire personalities.

As we learn the standards of our parents, religious authorities, neighbors, teachers, and other influential personalities, we may learn ways to behave which enhance our individuality or provide useful guides to action in the real world. On the other hand, we may have to deny our very flesh, our capacity to love ourselves or others, the power to defend ourselves. We may have to give up our peace of mind, our sense of being valuable people, our hope of some eternal peace and rest after death. All this martyrdom at the insistence of some people who demand compliance to their own standards of value without caring about the emotional consequences to the person they are guiding.

I am certainly not advocating the abolition of all standards of behavior and morality. However, even a casual look at the way people treat one another in the world will be strong evidence that the current ones have not been convincing guides for action, at the least, and perhaps have given justification for vast amounts of emotional and physical destruction.

Let us look at the guilty or valueless person—perhaps you yourself. The deepest feelings of sex or anger are forbidden. The sense of meeting new people or dealing as an equal with those you now know becomes a strain. They cannot accept me. I cannot be myself. I cannot be happy with others. I must reproach myself for being a human being with all of the drives and temptations. I must avoid deep relationships. I must keep people from stirring up my feelings. I must not talk to that attractive stranger because he will reject me. I must not change jobs because no other person will hire me. I cannot have a restful moment because I think of my sins.

There are a variety of disastrous effects of feeling guilt-ridden and thus valueless. Consider the *need for approval.* Relationships are formed and activities are directed not to obtaining pleasure but rather on the necessity of being liked, of being told that you are good. This is an extreme form of dependency. Thus, while some people restrict their feelings and relationships because they are guilty, others must alleviate their sense of guilt through always giving to others, pleasing others, through having the point of view that *survival depends on being a sycophant.* If you are obsequious you are self-destructive and lack emotional common sense.

Another unfortunate result of having a guilty conscience is either to accept abuse or even to provoke it. There are plenty of people in this life whose displaced hostilities, arrogance, and tortured self-esteem cause them to try to feel better at the expense of brutalizing others. They are looking for targets and you will do nicely. If you believe that you are a moral failure, that you do not deserve good treatment, that you are not a valuable, useful human being, then you will stand by and let yourself be further brutalized. You will continue to feel like a worthless piece of trash. Perhaps you will let others increase your belief that you are evil and condemned.

Some individuals actually provoke punishment or rejection. You must be sensitive to this in yourself or others. Do not play this game. One of the consequences of being treated like a guilty child is to believe you are one and then to try to alleviate this supreme sense of discomfort. Since we have a defective brain, instead of building up our ego through acts of love and productivity we accept the neurotic symptom. Individuals can provoke the anger of others or society's institutionalized punishment in order to be punished and thus relieved of their guilt. This is a telling argument against capital punishment—i.e., some people will murder in order to be executed themselves. However, this is a complex problem.

Some people act in an irritating way in order to be rejected. They seem to feel more comfortable with the idea that they are valueless. They must prove that they are not lovable. This is ridiculous, you say. Why would anybody do something so self-destructive as to provoke others to reject them, to reduce their self-esteem further? No one answer will cover all individuals, but sometimes the alternative is for these people to admit that they are worthwhile. But if they are worthwhile, then those who mistreated them, who told them that they were no good, were themselves evil or rotten people. We are so conditioned to assume that our parents or other authorities are right and we are wrong that we sometimes don't consider this possibility. We would feel guilty if we said to our parents, "You are mistreating me. Your values are wrong, your opinions misguided, your experience narrow. You lack a willingness to let me grow up and be my own person. You are not emotionally giving, loving, encouraging, supporting." To avoid this emotionally shattering conclusion, the person would rather provoke rejection, because to be accepted would be to prove that he is not guilty, not dirty, and not evil.

How can you recognize this attitude in yourself? Here is how some people verbalize it: "I never felt that I deserved anything." "I am not deserving or entitled." "I expected all supervisors to be authoritarian and beat me down." "If I don't accept the pain, there is the greater pain of loneliness." "I cry when I feel helpless and out of control."

Another consequence of guilt and low self-esteem is being susceptible to *emotional blackmail* and *guilt-provocation*. When we feel strong, when we believe that we deserve good treatment, when we are confident that we are considerate in our treatment of others, then a comfortable sense of self-assertion occurs. But should we doubt our basic morality, then we are the target of hostile, exploitative people who will use us for their own purposes.

Emotional blackmail is the threat to become angry or be unpleasant if the target does not act the way the blackmailer desires. "If you object to the way I treat you then I will kick, scream, have a tantrum, embarrass you, and in other ways cause you to act the way I want you to." Guilt-provocation is an equally insidious form of manipulation, implying that the other party is going to cause extreme pain, is a sinner, is a bad person. Emotional common sense dictates that after we understand our motives, if we feel that they are genuine and not designed to exploit others, then we resolutely tell these people that we will be the guide of our own actions and will not be affected by their concepts of how we should act. They are entitled to lead their own lives but will have to *pay the consequences for the way in which they treat you.*

Now that you have been offered some ways of recognizing your self-destructive trends, how can emotional common sense alleviate the discomfort?

It is important first of all that you develop *a new sense of values.* These may be within organized institutions, or they may represent those of people you esteem or perhaps a new creation which meets the test of your personal experiences. Many people change their confessors, stop visiting their guilt-provoking parents, join new religious denominations, or read extensively in philosophy. The important thing is to expose yourself to new values and ideas.

Secondly, you must learn to recognize the particular situations which provoke emotional discomfort in you or which play on your inadequacies. You may discover that particular people or classes of people or certain kinds of situations or locations make you anxious or remind you of guilt or inadequacy feelings. Now, you must associate these experiences with the original training that you had. Perhaps a certain teacher or supervisor reminds you of an earlier religious teacher or parent. Perhaps a person stirs up a sexual or anger impulse. At this point tell yourself that *you will live in the present.* You will evaluate every situation in terms of what it means for your present satisfaction or the realistic consequences. It is not my intention to suggest that you ought to be able

Going to church as a regular attender.

to do anything without regard for the consequence; rather, that anxiety and the rest of your emotional discomforts may be an *unrealistic evaluation* of what will happen if you do what you feel like doing.

Third, you will *temporarily have to disregard your feelings.* You will have to tell yourself that the feeling of guilt or anxiety or valuelessness is irrational. I am not saying that your emotional discomfort will rapidly or automatically disappear. Rather, by ceasing to restrict your activities you will have the opportunity to engage in new experiences, to test and learn new values, to meet new people, and basically to *experience yourself differently.* Above all, you will have to give up the idea that any failure is the beginning of a string of failures or of disaster.

Fourth, in case your anxiety and guilt are based on a *realistic estimate of your treatment of others* and how they feel about you, then it should be obvious that to destroy the well-being of others has been in essence self-destructive from your own point of view. If you don't give a damn about the feelings of others, this book isn't meant for you anyway.

There are some temporary measures which some people have found helpful while they are engaged in the long struggle against anxiety. Anxiety attacks can be controlled by relaxation exercises in which each part of the body is consciously directed to relax in turn; calling friends to get a feeling of closeness; physical exercise; planning something to do for tomorrow; typing free associations until the unconscious meaning of the anxiety or guilt comes clear; taking a tranquilizer without needing it; reading poetry; listening to music and watching TV.

Finally, if you realize that anxiety, guilt, and valuelessness are comprehensible, that they are an exaggerated reaction to old situations, that it is self-destructive to live in the past, then you can overcome it with a belief that you have a future with a sense of well-being.

10 Overcoming Loneliness and Deprivation

The twin pains of emotional deprivation and loneliness are not only the greatest burdens of many people; they can afflict even those who seem to be blessed by a large and active family. One only has to take into account the significant numbers of people who kill themselves, leaving behind parents, husband or wife, children, friends, to perceive the universality of this problem and the potential difficulty of experiencing closeness even in one's familiar milieu, to say nothing of a crowd.

It is useful to distinguish between emotional deprivation, loneliness, and alienation. *Deprivation* is the feeling of lack of love which people have when a parent or other loved one dies or is significantly rejecting or disinterested. *Loneliness* can occur at any age but is frequently found in older children and adults who believe that they are valueless or don't have the social skills to get close to others. *Alienation* is the experience of rejecting the values and other conditions of life, although it may originate in the experience of being rejected by others.

The need for contact with other members of our species is built into our nervous systems. Perhaps it is the stimulus for our very feeling of being alive and human. As young children we learn our self-image in part through seeing others. We also sense our bodies through being tossed by our parents as well as touched, fed, cleaned, warned, hurt, threatened, and so on by people. Both physical contact and emotional responsiveness add to the feeling of being loved. To the child, not to be caressed is equivalent to being told that he is unlovable. I have had many homosexual male patients who reported that they were never kissed or held by their fathers. Others have expressed other problems of relating when a parent died at an early age, or when one parent was physically present but seemingly indifferent to the child. One man said that he was angered by his father for not taking an interest; he didn't know if his father loved him or hated him.

Individuals who feel emotionally deprived have special problems subsequently. Often they do not feel self-assertive so that they cannot make friends or meet suitable mates with ease. They are the people who are so emotionally hungry that ordinary expressions of love, affection, and sex leave them unfulfilled. *Nothing is good enough.* Ask yourself whether people have complained about you that you are never satisfied, demand too much, or are just plain hard to please.

One of the oddest aspects of emotional deprivation is that many people who suffer from it do not know it! We pay such a price as children for being dependent that we will not admit it to ourselves as adults. Some people of course see themselves as totally incompetent so that in desperation they clutch onto others. If one clutchee cuts off from the emotional octopuslike tentacle and flees, the clutcher will soon find another victim.

On the other hand, there are individuals who see themselves as independent, perhaps even as givers, who experience deep frustration in their emotional needs. They pride themselves in their self-reliance and emotional generosity. Woe to them in a prolonged crisis. They are like the car that cannot get started on a wintry day because the battery is drained and the oil congealed. I know one woman who sprained her ankle on the street and was afraid to ask for help because she experienced as repellent the image of helpless old people.

To help others from the basis of your own deprivations can result in the healthy consequences reminding you even more

Being with others is not a matter of asking 'did we please them, but did I enjoy being with them, if so why, if not why,

Thus, there are twin dangers in feeling emotionally deprived which serve to create a sense of isolation and can lead to loneliness, a particularly unpleasant feeling for such a person. If the deprived person yields to his feelings, which are unreasonable from the point of view of those around him, then sensible people become defensive or flee, seeing him as inadequate, dependent, and insecure. If he denies his needs, then he does not experience life surrounded by people who are emotionally expressive and can nurture him. If at any time there is no one catering to the hungry one, he experiences a feeling that is dreaded: *loneliness.*

One of the most revealing aspects of discussing emotional problems with literally thousands of people in open Participation/Discussion groups that I lead was the central theme of loneliness in their lives. In the midst of New York City, which if you hadn't heard is pretty crowded, these people were lonely or feared loneliness. Emotional starvation in the midst of plenty. Fear of starvation in an ice-cream parlor.

Many people make profound decisions because of fear of loneliness, just as many others do for fear of anxiety. Loneliness is their most dreaded feeling. Mates, children, friends, neighbors are all tolerated when the plain facts are that these individuals are tearing away at their emotional flesh. These people dare not move away, are afraid to defend themselves against sadistic husbands and wives, or maintain noxious "love" relationships when they dare not lose their tormentor. Love, indeed. Cold, cringing, nauseating fear of being alone. A total lack of confidence that a more loving or accepting friend or mate can be found.

Fear of rejection is also characteristic of lonely, emotionally deprived people. Just the relatedness, the contact which will warm their spirits is hampered by an oversensitivity and lack of self-confidence. You believe that if you don't get too close you can't be rejected? Can you approach a stranger at a meeting who seems to have a compatible point of view? If unmarried, can you smile at a stranger across a crowded room? If a newcomer whom you might like wants to make contact, can you lend a helping

vividly of your deprivation. So many refuse to be helpful, because they cannot deal with this further dimension of pain.

hand? No? Then you are self-destructive and need all the help you can get.

Among the self-destructive ways of avoiding rejection and loneliness are having sex with total strangers in order to have a companion, always mixing with a crowd so that the feared intimacy is not risked, or "running around town to oases to get emotional support." You may also deceive yourself into believing that a cold, poor relationship is valuable.

Fear of commitment is also frequently experienced by lonely, emotionally deprived people. They do not see themselves as strong enough to protect themselves from the stresses of relationships. Perhaps they feel that they are so cold that the other person's reasonable needs for warmth will completely deplete them. Frequently the turmoil of their households which led to their own deprivation caused them to fear entering into a relationship which would repeat the pain. Thus the very warmth which would relieve their misery represents a tender trap of commitment and causes them to become anxious and run away or spoil a good experience.

A closely related problem is *alienation*. To feel different from one's surroundings, to be unable to relate to people, events, and institutions meaningfully, to feel emotionally distant from everything and everyone is a guarantee of loneliness, deprivation, and feelings of rejection. Alienation is sometimes a necessary defense against oppression. A member of an oppressed minority forced to reside among those who have contempt and hatred for him maintains a better adjustment for feeling distant from his tormentors. However, some people feel alienated as a neurotic defense against feelings of insufficiency. Here it takes the form of superiority feelings. After all, "only pagans, apes, or barbarians could treat me the way they did." Such attitudes are frequently developed by bullied or scorned children and isolate them even after they have the strength and mobility to surround themselves with friendly faces. Others become alienated because of narrow-minded parents and teachers who did not educate them to the differences between cultures, to the valid customs of other groups, to techniques of

understanding people in order to communicate with them as
equals on the basis of shared humanity. To such unfortunates, all
of the world except for a few people with whom they group are
permanently outsiders.

What are the symptoms of alienation? To be alienated is to be
unable to enjoy meeting new people; to operate on the periphery
of events; to see life as "sliding through a nightmare, with nothing
real"; to feel "boxed in and turned off"; "having to have a plastic
personality in order to survive"; to lack common interests with
others. The symptoms fit you? Don't give up. They're curable.

An important solution of the problem of loneliness, deprivation,
and alienation is *making and keeping friends*. This may come as
a surprise to those of you who feel that a love relationship is what
you really need, preferably an unrealistic, idealized, romantic,
sloppy, epic musical with a cast of thousands directed by Cecil B.
De Mille. Forget it. These are merely adolescent fantasies you
developed when that little girl went to the junior prom with the
gorilla from the other class, or when those pimples on your face
convinced you that you would go through life unloved.

Making and keeping friends is a psychologically important factor in its own right. It creates an atmosphere in which we can
avoid the worst effects of stress and its emotional discomforts and
also create a pleasant frame of mind in which we can face other
problems. Friendship will by itself help to overcome tendencies to
deprivation, loneliness, and alienation. While friends are not a
complete substitute for a loving physical relationship, they create
some feelings of satisfaction which can tide one over until such a
closeness is achieved.

I asked a large group of people what characteristics they required in their friends. Check their answers so that you can compare them with your own requirements and see also whether you
can meet the needs of others: non-competitiveness; sensitivity;
reliability; acceptance; initiative; commitment; support; kindness;
generosity; sincerity; not pretending the other person is something he's not; understanding in the face of depression; having

common interests; rapport or tolerance for each other's crazy ways; honesty; communication on a real level; getting something not possible from someone else.

There are several key issues in making and keeping friends: Taking the initiative to form the relationship; the optimal degree of closeness; giving and taking; honesty and criticism; trust; and shared activities.

It should be obvious that no friendship can be started without one or both individuals taking the initiative and in some manner expressing interest. This is obviously a matter both of good judgment (that the other party is interested) and taking a risk. Very likely some approaches are not welcomed either because of the ineptitude of the initiator or because he or she is perceived as having too radically different values or life style from the other party. The possible nature of rejection should be considered and added to one's stock of worldly wisdom to avoid making similar mistakes in the future. This, however, is not an invitation to cowardice. Repeat: If you remain as cowardly as you have proved to be in the past, you will be stuck with deprivation.

The ultimate degree of closeness which is achieved and the speed with which it is approached are two of the most important considerations in forming a friendship. It is a matter of frequent observation that strangers traveling together exchange the most intimate revelations and then split, signifying that the maximum of intimacy is no proof of friendship and may signify nothing. On the contrary, I have known individuals with whom I would have liked to have friendly contact flee from me after too deep a personal revelation on their part. They experienced shame, although I myself did not look at them critically. Therefore, as in all forms of human relationships, it is important to be aware of the other person's reactions to your feelings and responses. Be sensitive to the other person's possible discomfort at your expression of feelings and experiences or to a front you put up which keeps you from being known.

Giving and taking are important parts of friendship. I know of one relationship (you can decide for yourself whether it was a friendship) where two men played chess on a weekly basis for twenty years. At the end of that time they ceased the game and never saw each other again. They entertained each other without commitment, then called it quits. We have discussed before some of the origins and effects of excessive dependence or clutching, and this topic is important enough to be developed further. Let us consider the psychology of being a "giver." To some individuals, this is a vital role, and they feel very uncomfortable if they cannot assume it. They are probably covering up deep feelings of inadequacy. They (you) can be recognized by being excessive tippers, never letting the other person pick up the bill, throwing overly lavish parties, selecting as companions deprived people, and so forth. What are the effects of this compulsive kind of behavior? The person who said "If you care for somebody it's not draining" is probably in the minority. More frequent are such comments as "Always the crying shoulder"; "It's good to be giving, but after five years it's too much"; "What am I getting out of it"; "You put yourself in an inferior position by always being a sounding board"; "I'm tired of being told how good I am by people who benefited and went to someone else."

Let us consider the reactions of people to "takers": "Making her feel good made a wreck out of me, so I split"; "The most famous giver's reward was in heaven"; "A taker in giver's clothing"; "Takers are selfish and insensitive." If you are a taker, beware. You will be seen through and rejected, having then to clutch onto someone else. Have a heart! Should you be a giver, learn to recognize the takers. They are sometimes the underprivileged of life. Sometimes they are people who are trained to exploit others through having been spoiled or by the training and example of selfish parents. Frequently they are individuals who are going through a traumatic, stressful period because of some separation or loss of a loved person on whom they were dependent, and anybody is game to be shot down for their needs. *There is a difference between having compassion and being a sucker.*

What, then, is an approach to giving and taking which shows emotional common sense? First, you have to be prepared to ask, and you have to be willing to accept warmth in order to enjoy it. Secondly, material and emotional gifts are not completely interchangeable. Be aware of this both as offerer and recipient. Third, to give gifts is no guarantee of stability—that is, be aware of all facets of the relationship and events in the other person's life. Do not accept gifts of great value, knowing you feel like separating, unless you are a rotter or enjoy big, sordid scenes. Fourth, expressing concern is not the same as remedying a situation. Whether you or your friend is in the position of giver or taker, realistic considerations may require realistic assistance, not just expression of feelings. Fifth, be appreciative. If you can't learn to say thank you nicely without minimizing the offering and feelings of the other party, discipline yourself to do so. Sixth, learn the difference between realistic and unrealistic obligations. To expect someone to be obligated to you when he does not experience this is to make demands and be disillusioned by the breakup of the friendship. Neither feel obliged to meet others' expectations of you nor demand that others meet your expectations. Let everyone live his own life, but simply be alert to expressions of emotional generosity freely offered.

Honesty and constructive criticism are certainly part of friendship, yet more friendships are destroyed by mishandling them than by any other experience. The chief problem is that many people cannot recognize the difference between honest helpfulness on the one hand and degrading put-downs on the other. Even a helpful comment, a mildly worded criticism can be exaggerated by an overly sensitive person to be a malicious attempt to hurt. On the other hand, the feeling of superiority, the intention of maintaining the other person in an inferior position, can be in the guise of an attempt to help. What is probably needed is a sense of timing. The person who is in trouble wants emotional support and not criticism. Oh, you insist on telling the truth at all times? Well, clod, no wonder you have no friends. When the crisis is over, then there is time to approach your friend in a gentle, querying manner, perhaps offering an impression, suggesting that he didn't foresee the consequences of certain actions—certainly not implying stupidity, basic inferiority which couldn't be helped, and so on. Sympathy and regrets are always in order, even if the results could have been foretold in advance. If you feel that you have gently and honestly tried to help the other person overcome some weakness or fault and the result is that you are snapped at, you must explore whether you have really been offensive or your friend "just can't take it" and then act according to your own needs.

What about receiving criticism? Frankly, I hate being criticized. However, I have disciplined myself to listen to it, at least momentarily. To reject criticism is possibly to lose valuable information which can help you to overcome self-destructive behavior. However, when a person is constantly critical, then one risks having one's good spirits and morale ruined, and it is wise to separate yourself firmly from the abrasive personality who values his hostility more than your good will. Also, you must become aware that if you are excessively sensitive, it is an example of your defective brain misleading you. After all, what you are still doing is blocking out the hostility of parents and other people in your early life instead of relating to the current world as it is.

Two of the most beautiful feelings in friendship are trust and reliability. Friend will offer friend the confidence that his interests will be respected. This may mean not breaking confidence, not abusing or criticizing the other person in public, certainly not taking away one's money, mate, or job. I personally value reliability most highly. It is my philosophy not to deal with unreliable individuals no matter what their other values. If someone does not fulfill a promise or other genuine obligation, makes a habit of breaking appointments (particularly without letting me know in advance), does not return money, he does not get a further chance. Let others support his delinquency. My life is too valuable to me.

Finally, what kind of activities does one engage in with friends?

As one person put it, "What do you do after you've said hello?" It is probably impossible to form a firm friendship without some common interests. They may be purely talk and intellectual exchange. Perhaps they may represent activities such as whoring, fishing, drinking, chess, sports, or enjoying art or music together. But friendship implies some mutually fulfilled need. Since with your complex mind you have a variety of preferred activities, it may be good emotional common sense to have a variety of friends. With some of them you will seek sexual release, with others you will attend lectures, and with still others you will complain about how life has been mistreating you.

Should you have some feelings of vulnerability which will impair your ability to make friends, let me share some ideas that have proven helpful to others: Share hobbies; ask for what you want; use humor to get out of yourself and be with people; refuse to accept derogatory comments as valid; do those things which increase self-esteem; be self-determining; take chances—by evaluating the consequences you will generally find that the risks are minimal; analyze what you have been doing and avoid activities which ensure rejection; stop creating parental figures; take an interest in others; understand the motives of others; experience each situation as separate rather than accumulating rejections; in general, be independent.

These simple aids emphasize that others should not determine our value, that since occasional rejections are inevitable they should not be taken seriously, and that our feelings of valuelessness are inaccurate and ridiculous. Nevertheless, *if we want to feel valuable, we must step out and do something positive.* In addition, *we must be simultaneously aware of both our needs and those of our intended friend.*

By following with zeal the knowledge and precepts offered in this chapter, you will have a fighting chance to overcome your feelings of emotional emptiness. Now let us consider some complex problems which are presented in the next chapter.

11 Reducing Interpersonal Antagonism

I approached the writing of this chapter with some trepidation and sense of frustration. Anger is so pervasive in the world, people are so irrational in their selection of targets, the expression of it so unpredictable and devious that it seems like a hopeless task to do something about it.

People like being angry; they enjoy personal or institutionalized murder. They think nothing of hurting each other's feelings and are too proud to make up the damage, and in a variety of ways they justify the rottenest parts of human nature. Just remember, it is human nature to be angry, and *don't let any stupid people tell you that people are inherently good.* This is a lot of nonsense. *People are born not good, not bad, but infantile.* As they grow up, they become assailed by circumstances, some of which we have discussed and others of which you are aware. Because of the inefficiency of the brain, the experiences of anger affect the way we think about ourselves, our concepts of individuals and people in general, and how we solve problems and cope with stress. Thus, the capacity for anger, which is built into our nervous system as a residual of the primitive man's need to defend himself, is a living, grasping, manipulating part of everybody's personality. This includes you. It is my belief that anger plays as large a role, and probably a larger one, in shaping personality than genital sexuality.

Since some of these assertions are unpopular, I suggest that you make some efforts to evaluate them for yourself. For example, you might read *Violence and the Brain*, by V. H. Mark and F. R. Ervin, a paperback accessible to the layman's understanding, and *The Emotional Stress of War, Violence, and Peace*, edited by myself. Since anger and violence pose the greatest dangers of all to yourself and anything you hold dear, don't be lazy. Learn about them.

To really get an appreciation of the nature of anger, it is necessary to compare ourselves to a despised species, the wild rat. Along with other so-called educated people, I assumed that this beast was widely separated in evolution from the proud family of mankind. Thus the following paleontological data must be remembered when we consider Lorenz's description of rat behavior. A. E. Wood, in "Interrelations of Humans, Dogs, and Rodents," published in *Science*, 1972, asserts that "From the fossil record, it appears fairly certain that rodents and primates are more closely related to each other than either is to carnivores." K. Lorenz, in *On Aggression*, gives us a perspective on the biological basis for our behavior to each other: "In their behavior towards members of their own community . . . [rats] are models of social virtue; but they change into horrible brutes as soon as they encounter members of any other society of their own species. . . . Constant warfare between large neighboring families of rats must exert a huge selection pressure in the direction of an ever increasing ability to fight. . . ."

It will be useful to you to have a clear-cut understanding of the various aspects of anger. I differentiate between *anger* (which is a feeling), *hostility* (which is behavior based on anger), and *aggression* (which is a more inclusive term implying anger, hostility, a high degree of intensity, and a need to master a situation).

Let us consider the previous assertion that anger is part of our biological heritage, which is another way of saying that *anger is not learned*. One has only to observe a frustrated infant to know that it arrived on this planet ready to do battle with its enemies as soon as it could identify or misidentify them. What is learned is the *means of expressing anger* and the *targets for anger*. You have probably been taught that when people behave a certain way it is appropriate for you to punish them or perhaps to destroy them completely. You have probably not been taught that it is important to make sure that you are punishing the right person and that maybe you were just a little bit to blame yourself for starting the fight. If you were taught this at all, the chances are that your mentors went overboard in the opposite direction, telling you that it is naughty to fight and otherwise hampering you in defending your true interests in a healthy way.

Another problem in the experience and expression of anger is that it tends to be aroused by or to accompany many other basic feelings and drives. Anger accompanies sexuality. In fact, the locale for its arousal in the brain is close to those centers which also integrate sex and orality. Wilhelm Stekel, in *Sadism and Masochism*, went so far as to state that "there is no cruelty not toned with sexual pleasure. . . . Man is cruel for the sake of the pleasure which the barbarous act produces." Thus, the tendency for sex and anger to be simultaneously aroused is likely to result in their mutual reinforcement, or being associated and expressed together.

Anger is also aroused by emotional pain and humiliation. And the belief that our power is curbed makes us angry. Since inferiority feelings are a widespread form of emotional discomfort, the tendency to compensate for them through humiliating others, and a comparable degree of oversensitivity and vulnerability, are both very common causes of anger.

Frustrated dependency needs are also experienced as a direct aggressive attack. Since dependency needs are basic to all people, and since we do not always grow and live in an atmosphere of warmth, the possibilities of having anger aroused are infinite. Oddly enough, some authors have noted that a certain amount of frustration is necessary for development; *children need some op-*

position from their parents. While excessive opposition creates rage, a minimal amount permits the child to grow toward strength and independence. This also helps to account for the sense of loss when a passionate opponent dies: *Part of our identity is determined by who our enemies are!*

Even *anxiety* is a source of aggression. Theodor Reik claims that hatred is experienced only for objects one fears. Therefore, certain crimes and suicides are explainable as attempts to reduce anxiety. Some people become innocent victims because aggression, as well as sexuality, reduces tension, or because of an irrational fear aroused by the person or the group he represents. Further, since anxiety is related to fear of punishment, it seems that our personal guilt can make somebody else pay for our own misdoings if we provoke authority into punishing us by attacking an innocent victim.

I would like to comment briefly and incompletely on some developmental aspects of anger and how it influences whom we attack irrationally. By an *irrational target* I mean one that is either not the original source of our anger or one to which the angry response is excessive or one which is attacked long after the original provocation. First, it seems most likely that the personal experience of being brutalized, or watching vicious or justified attacks on others, makes children prone to violence. Not only does "violence beget violence," but the model of violence encourages children immediately and subsequently to be violent or justify its use by others. Thus child abusers and some creators of popular media to which children are exposed are in my opinion *criminals in the same category.* It is probably justified to have all individuals educated to the extent and nature of violence so that they may take intelligent steps to defend themselves and as citizens encourage appropriate action by responsible public and private agencies. It is something entirely different to glorify or show explicit scenes and other descriptions of sadism. Children are impressionable. They are likely to assume that what they have experienced is the nature of the world, and thus to react with either intense anxiety or to make plans to take vicious retribution against others. In any event, they and society will pay for years and generations to come. When children are treated with brutality by parents, siblings, or others, this affects their self-image and also their fantasies. These mental images, which I have called identification nuclei, have a content, a feeling (often unpleasant), a tendency toward activity to reduce the unpleasant feeling, relevant targets to whom it will be expressed, and conditions for its release. The brutalization or other mistreatment of children may have a variety of effects. It may make the child feel weak, inadequate and/or vengeful. Or the child may identify with the aggressive parents (Anna Freud's concept): "By impersonating the aggressor . . . the child transforms himself from the person threatened into the person who makes the threat."

Another effect of mistreatment of a child is to cause him to create fantasies of vengeance. Thus, when he is older, on meeting people who remind him of those who he felt bullied him when he was young and vulnerable, he acts out his fantasies on innocent victims. From mistreatment we often learn not compassion but rather revenge.

A different kind of fantasy, one which serves as a lock-and-key relationship to the above, is the fantasy of the rescuing, nurturing adult who will treat the child as he really deserves being treated. This is sometimes the origin of the compulsive giving that we have discussed. The formerly frustrated child, now a would-be giver, selects some depriving *ungiving* ally, one who will frustrate and punish, and then proceeds to wheedle and plead for satisfaction. But this satisfaction is not to be obtained in reality; it is to obtain vindication for his lack of dignity and value years ago when he was a child. Thus these two types of people meet each other with joy, and the famous sado-masochistic relationship is born. For each brute there is a willing victim.

Another insidious form of irrational target selection in adult relationships I have described as "Hostile Identification with Pain-inflicting Parents" (Parker, 1972a). I became aware in my practice of group psychotherapy that particular patients would often attack others for having certain traits. Since I knew the aggressor, after a while I saw a pattern in which he picked a target who had traits which he himself had. Then I perceived that the despised trait which "justified" the attack was one which was *possessed by a parent and experienced by the aggressor as very painful.* Thus, victim, aggressor, and pain-inflicting parent all had the same characteristic. Oddly enough, the victim of the attack generally had not provoked the aggression directly. In this way, the sins of the parents are repeated by the children through unprovoked hostility to others.

Among the examples of identification with pain-inflicting parents that I have described were the tendency to embarrass others, violence, passivity, critical attitude, sarcasm, and provocativeness. The reader might find it useful to consider what characteristics of his parents pained him the most, and to determine whether he not only has assumed these activities but also is extremely critical of others who are just like him and dear old Dad or Mom.

Again, let me repeat: Anger is very complicated, and the means of dealing with it are multitudinous. This review is only to alert you to the tendency you have to pick irrational targets for your anger and to warn you not to permit yourself to be a target for others.

What are some of the *circumstances that make people angry?* By reviewing this list you can become more sensitive to the feelings (and weak points) of others, and perhaps become aware that you yourself are overly sensitive or vulnerable. Individuals have experienced or observed anger for some of these reasons: frustration at being teased; not being liked; having one's arguments sidetracked; lack of respect; lack of honesty; having one's mind read (assumptions about what you are thinking); overgeneralizing; someone's lack of conformity to society; being stereotyped; not being seen as a human being; being told what one should do; inflexibility in a romantic argument; being insulted; being used as a sounding board, but the confider doesn't listen to your reply;

suffering a critical, holier-than-thou attitude; not being permitted to express anger; helplessness; inadequacy; being deceived; frustrating real or unreal expectations from others; crowding; someone not understanding another's objectives; not reacting the way others do; being ignored; rejection; discourtesy; deception. A transit worker was angry when little old ladies didn't pay their fare!

Any of these situations are understandable in terms of direct humiliation or attack or frustration. In some cases the angry feelings might not be experienced by less vulnerable people, but there is a basic honesty about the experience.

Often, however, anger is used as a manipulative "game" to obtain selfish ends. The aggressor is not angry but pretends to be so in order to obtain some devious goal. For example, a person who is ashamed to *terminate a relationship* directly may pretend to have a temper tantrum in order to provoke the other party into taking responsibility for the separation. Anger may be used to *avoid confrontation* concerning the real nature of a person's behavior. One person may become angry if accused of being cruel. Other individuals use *emotional blackmail* (see p. 90). If they are frustrated they work themselves into a frightening rage until they get what they want. *Teasing* is a poorly recognized technique for expressing hostility and humiliating a weaker target.

Emotional common sense demands that if you use these techniques, you should learn to assert yourself in a less infantile way. The fruit of this kind of behavior is to be hated or treated with contempt. However, if you are a victim, then your dignity requires that you not put up with it in a single further instance. Many such bullies require to be put in their place. They really are inviting punishment and laugh at you for not seeing through their games and their real need to be treated as the guilty people they experience themselves to be. Take no actions based on someone's emotional blackmail. Let them be furious, let them threaten suicide, accuse you of being the cause of their death, and so on. Look them in the eye and inform them that since everyone has to die, you respect their strength to choose the time and place of their own death. If the teaser will not cease and is too strong to be assaulted, *get rid of him or her.* The odious skunk who avoids criticism through outbursts of anger ought to be permitted to be infantile and then politely told what a creep he is. Let him be angry; it's his privilege.

Another kind of manipulation is telling people when it is acceptable for them to be angry, to shape their feelings as it were. This is more devious than the different parental styles used to control children referred to in Chapter 8. The goal is obviously the same: Let me do what I want but also let me get away with it because I will make you feel guilty or socially inadequate if you become angry with me. Learn to recognize this straitjacket for your feelings: "How can you be angry with your mother?"; "Crying is a cop-out"; "It's O.K. for you to be angry, but don't show it here"; (during a political discussion, while in a Jewish couple's home) "I'm tired of hearing about the Jews killed in Europe"; (principal to supervisor) "You shouldn't be angry at that subordinate."

Still another kind of manipulation is to provoke anger needlessly. This is characteristic of people who are in close relationships, and it is a pattern that ought to be stamped out by either self-discipline in keeping one's mouth shut, refusing to start or continue the fight, psychotherapy, or firmly ceasing the relationship if nothing else helps. Some examples would be a husband telling his wife about anything he does that makes him feel guilty. Consider the mother who ceaselessly asks her daughter about all of her activities. Or the employee who comes to work late repeatedly after being informed that this is intolerable to the higher-ups. Insistence on "having the last word" or hammering home the last nail is intolerable. The real motive is to justify the breakup of the relationship, or to obtain punishment for guilt, or to dominate, even though the basis sometimes derives from earlier, irrelevant situations.

After all of this material on the harmful effects of anger (and we have hardly begun) you may ask, "Is it ever justified to express anger?" The answer is that it is certainly justified to express anger, but as in a lot of human relationships, you will have to face the consequences. It is immoral to accept the teachings of some so-called gurus who emphasize that you must always express your feelings. Yet there are emotional situations in which your well-being demands that you express your anger. I once asked a group of twenty-eight people if they had ever saved a relationship by not expressing their anger and not one said yes. This is a vital point. Some people hold back their perfectly justified anger through fear of being left alone. This is an example of making important decisions because loneliness is dreaded as excruciating. Others deceive themselves by believing that to be angry and to show it is immature. Some believe that they must be rational and not show feelings. Therefore they hold back their anger to avoid being considered unintelligent or irrational.

It is a serious, damaging condition not to be able to express anger. In the first place, to hold back anger means to run the risk of such psychosomatic conditions as high blood pressure and muscular fatigue. Secondly, while there are other ways of coping with problems, sometimes to hold back anger results in an avoidance of the real issues between people. Third, holding back anger does not eliminate it. It seems to accumulate and your anger becomes expressed in irrelevant ways harmful to your best interests. It can be displaced to other people. To use a classic example, an employer bawls out a man, who in turn abuses his wife, who hits the kid, who pulls the kitty's tail. Fourth, holding anger back makes some issues become larger than they really are as we ruminate about all the injustices that are perpetrated on us. Fifth, the philosophy "peace at any price" doesn't work: To hoard feelings is to invite a condition of "fermenting anger." This is an explosive brew and shows itself in rage, separation, and/or depression. Don't follow the advice of this man: "If you tell somebody off after twenty years they will think you've gone off your rocker." Finally, to express anger is to give the other person some indication of your feelings, that you are alive, that you care. Sometimes the lover or friend or mate feels that you are indifferent if "anything goes." He can be motivated to change the way he acts if he knows that it is upsetting.

Let us then consider some of the ways in which anger can be expressed usefully or without unnecessary harm to human relationships. It is important to understand what is making you angry. Therefore, you should try to determine whether the other person has a motive for degrading or harming you. You should try to see if there is a misunderstanding or whether the other person's behavior is reasonable or acceptable by his own standards and your training is such that you become provoked. Here there are some grounds for discussion. Perhaps no harm is intended and you are overly sensitive. In any event, some discussion is probably in order to clarify the issues and take further action. It is also important to consider the other person's feelings. When you are angry, if you are excessively accusatory, you will make the situation worse. There is a difference between "I am angry at the way you are treating me" and "You are no good." Unless you wish to terminate the relationship, don't automatically escalate your anger to that kind of exaggeration known as abuse. You ought to make it clear that you value the person but can't stand only part of him or her. By pointing out some of the hurtful behavior, you are not "wiping out" your partner. Perhaps it would be useful if you indicated that you want to improve matters and are not interested in criticism or humiliation of the other person. Remember that you don't (in most cases) hate that person completely. People who are angry tend either to magnify it or minimize it, and at the point of expressing it you can certainly either shape the course of the relationship or see how the other person reacts to being told that he is making you angry.

Another consideration is trying to find out what you personally have contributed to the situation. It is true that at a given time you may be furious at what has been done, but, my self-destructive friend, I know you. You are provocative and don't deny it. Ask the other person what he is angry about. Also find out if there is a repetitive element in the situations which make you angry to determine whether your own sensitivities have been on overtime or you have been unwittingly provocative in stirring up the natives. Make sure that the communications have been clear, because the whole battle may be caused by a misunderstanding.

What do people do when they are angry and they can't do something about it? Some chop wood, swim, jog, beat on pillows, go into the bathroom and scream, open the windows and scream.

I think that we might conclude this chapter on anger with the following *emotional common sense criteria for appropriate expression of anger:*

1. *Select the right target.* Make sure the person you express your anger at is the one who provoked you. Don't have a fight with your wife and then provoke a foreign war.

2. *Monitor the amount of anger.* Be certain that the response fits the provocation. Very likely neither rage nor relative acceptance is appropriate.

3. *Express your feelings in a timely way.* It is probably better to come out with it when you understand yourself and the situation than to wait a long time while the wounds fester and the real situation becomes forgotten or distorted.

Anger exists; it is built into the nervous system. Learn about it so that it doesn't destroy you.

12 *Handling Depression*

Depression is one of the most complicated and painful afflictions man suffers from. In its mildest forms it ruins one's good spirits and productivity. At its extreme it leads to determined, resourceful, and successful attempts to destroy one's own life. More than most conditions, depression is a crisis in the life of the sufferer, the family, and the therapist.

Since there are many kinds of depression and some of them are sufficiently severe to require hospitalization, I will address my comments to the form that many people experience which may be called unhappiness or dejection. I will also try to clarify the nature and risk of suicide, which is a solution considered by many people and attempted by enough to be considered a major cause of death.

The description of their own feelings by participants in a group discussion of depression is a suitable introduction: "Weak; hurt; sleepy; slowed down; paralyzed; unable to do anything; disinterested in anything but my own problems; hopeless; helpless; insurmountable problems; self-condemnatory; fear of the mood continuing."

By understanding the origin of depression and how it affects one's family and companions, it is possible to overcome it more

114

rapidly. However, it must be pointed out that depression seems in *some cases to be caused by medical illnesses.* I myself lost a friend through a suicidal depression after she had many months of suffering from a thyroid condition that had not been diagnosed. Disorders of other endocrine glands, arteriosclerosis, and alcoholism are but some of the pathological conditions that cause depression. Further, there seems to be an additional entity called *endogenous depression* (physiologically based) as opposed to *exogenous depression* (reaction to psychological events). Thus, the existence of a long and unexplained depression calls for a medical examination by a thorough, psychologically oriented physician.

Nevertheless, most feelings of depression are based on a person's reactions to his life's experiences. It has been established that some people are prone to depression because of experiences of loss or temporary separation from their parents early in life. The period of separation need not have been very long. I can think of one patient who had a brief hospitalization during which she was put in an oxygen tent and thus not able to be with her parents, particularly her father. He was a distant person, and a visit at this time might have been particularly meaningful to her. She suffers from depression and discomfort when even temporarily separated from her husband. When her father died, she took over the responsibility for his burial from her mother. She expressed so little grief that I put her under hypnosis to let her express her feelings. Then she wailed about wanting her father's love and her pain at watching him die—also while in an oxygen tent.

Thus, the key to understanding depression is the *sense of loss.* The loss may be of a person—child, spouse, lover—or it may be of an abstraction such as prestige, status, or hope of success. Paradoxically, some people become depressed when they are promoted or otherwise successful. An associated experience in depression is the *inability to express anger at somebody important.* Sometimes the anger is experienced as due to humiliation—for example, by the employer, mate, or parent whom we can't talk back to. Then the anger is *internalized* or turned inward on ourselves. Sometimes the depression which follows a death or separation is internalized because we are angry at the person for departing and he is obviously not there to experience our rage.

It is often observable that a *sense of guilt accompanies depression*. It is as though the depressed person is reproaching himself. Such people often have very strict superegos or consciences. If they have failed, then they feel guilty for violating their high standards. Obviously this is one of the worst gifts that a parent can endow a child with: standards high enough to ensure certain failure. This tendency toward self-reproach also helps us to explain the frequent examples of depression following success. To some people, being promoted or otherwise achieving recognition is the emotional equivalent of destroying their relationship with their parents. Thus they believe emotionally, because of unconscious fantasies, that they no longer have parents on whom they can depend. Other people believe that success can only occur through the hostile destruction of opponents. To be successful is to them proof that they have given in to their sadism, and they then reproach themselves for being rotten.

At this point we can consider the effects on other people due to the unconscious experiences of the depressed person. Since the latter often feels guilt and reproaches himself, then others are motivated to help him, reassure him, make him feel better. This is certainly a worthy effort, as anybody will say if they have ever felt really depressed. In some cases, it does not seem to work because the victim of depression is simply getting too much gain out of the attentions of others. If you have been suffering from a long depression, then you ought to consider the possibility that its duration has been augmented by the hope that others will be nicer to you than they would ordinarily. The feeling of depression is too high a price to pay for the rewards of manipulation! On the other hand, should somebody close to you be suffering from depression, then you must be alert to the possibility that you will become emotionally involved in ways beyond your normal degree of concern. The depression, assuming that it does not have a medical origin, may arouse your intensive intervention for a variety of reasons. Such people sometimes need reassurance because they experience with extra intensity due to early experiences of losses of people or status. Sometimes a depression is a signal to the people around one that they have not met the needs of the person or are not letting him express his feelings of anger or love. The feelings of depression are used to provoke guilt and sympathy in place of a direct statement requesting support.

When confronted by a situation like this, you have a number of alternatives but ought to start with an exploration of your relationship with the depressed person. Perhaps he has a legitimate claim upon your affection and attention, and you have unwittingly been neglectful. On the other hand, some people make a lifelong habit of making emotional demands, and the proper response is to get a psychotherapeutic consultation for them. Should the depressed person refuse this, then there is justification for acting independently and avoiding being manipulated.

All of the feelings of depression are magnified in the suicidal person—expectation that the pain will go on forever, futility, hopelessness, withdrawal, guilt, self-reproach, and so forth. At one time it was believed that "the person who talks about suicide will never commit it." *This is positively inaccurate.* The person who talks about suicide may be giving a message to anyone who will listen. What your response is will be determined by your relationship and your personality, but I hope that you will not stand idly by while someone you cherish and value kills himself or herself because *no one listened, so it appeared that no one cared.* Suicide is characterized by discouragement, disillusionment, and disappointment. It is motivated by the wish to destroy some hated part of one's personality, hostility toward some other person who has become a part of one's personality and fantasy life (introjected), a desire for reunion with a loved person who is dead, or a need to expiate for guilt. A particular crisis often arises around the fortieth year, when the need for fulfillment in love and vocation seems to be challenged seriously.

The safest course to take if you have serious suicidal feelings or someone you care about has them is to go into psychotherapy. Even hospitalization with its relief from stress might be indicated. In these circumstances, there is no need to suffer emotional pain needlessly. Certainly, your attention should be directed *immediately* to the final chapter in this book on selecting a competent psychotherapist. Suicide seems most frequent in white men, particularly those who are single, widowed or divorced.

Since the goal of this book is to enable you personally to handle your affairs with emotional common sense, let us look at the problem of recognizing and alleviating depression. While depression is sometimes a readily recognizable feeling of deadness, frozenness, or unhappiness, it can be hidden. Some people recognize depression through feeling that they have no future, or are let down after an intensely unhappy experience, or see themselves as goalless or having lost mastery, or have nothing to look forward to. There is a feeling of inner emptiness and inactivity, accompanied by a loss of interest, initiative, and energy. Lonely weekends or holiday evenings when it is believed that everyone else is enjoying time spent with family or friends are particularly troublesome. Depression sometimes reveals itself as a "cold" when unhappiness might be expected after a particular experience. The symptom of early-morning awakening is a frequent sign of a depressive experience. Some people hide depressed feelings through overindulgence in sex, or burying themselves in work. Reckless driving often reveals self-destructive or suicidal trends. Please, if you wish to die and you don't want any help, go quietly. Do not kill others along with yourself on the highway, and by all means do not tie up the New York City subway system by jumping in front of a train during the rush hour.

Once you have become aware that you are suffering from depression, it is now appropriate to determine what emotional stress or other causes brought it on. Here are some of the probable causes of depression: loss of a loved one or rejection in love; loss of one's job; suppressed rage or anger; bodily injury; fatigue;

The vividness + intensity of our choice.

chemical imbalance; excessively high goals which create frustration and expected failure. These in turn may lead to depression
symptoms, some of which spiral downward and intertwine with
each other to cause even deeper depression. Causes lead to symptoms and are often the reason for further emotional stress. Some
of the causes are environmental; some come from within the person himself.

Here, gathered from members of Participation/Discussion
groups I have led, are some of these symptomatic feelings: fear
that you will ultimately be unable to do what you would like to;
feeling that life is meaningless; that alternatives are worthless; not
having any goals; alienation—feeling that you don't belong; not
feeling connected even though you can socialize; feeling all alone,
with nobody in the world interested in you; having nobody to tell
your problems to; feeling that your brothers and sisters get more
attention from your parents than you do; inability to communicate
your feelings; having a feeling of valuelessness, of purposelessness;
your circumstances are beyond your control; some of your goals
remove you from people; you feel unable to achieve anything
worthwhile; you use other people as standards. There are undoubtedly many more causes of depression and feelings which
accompany depression.

Let's see what we can do to overcome depression. A key is to
remember what the opposite of depression is. Since it leads to
reduced activity, its opposite and antidote is more activity—if you
can rouse yourself to try it. There are many things you can do that
will help overcome feelings of pain, loss, valuelessness—provided,
of course, that you want to feel better, to be happier and not to
wallow in your misery. Many people actually do almost enjoy their
depression, or seem to. At least one person I know feels that he
helped himself begin to get over a long period of depression when
he said to himself, "Stupid, if *you* want to live like that, go on and
do it! *I'm* not going to stand for it any more."

An essential strategy of overcoming depression is in understanding the hurtful parts of the past and renouncing them. Enjoy

Identification of what you like! — count + chair insard

friends—if you feel you have any at this point. Do something useful or at least amusing, in sports, music, reading, painting, crossword puzzles, dancing, cooking, listening to music, or following any hobby.

Other specific activities that have proved to be of value include physical exercise; reaching out to people by calling someone with whom you can share your feelings; going to work or changing one's job (often difficult to do as you feel in no mood to try to do a "selling job" to a potential employer); changing activities so as to enhance self-esteem; taking more risks in order to obtain greater gratification in employment and love; seeing parents and/or lover more realistically; fighting with a pillow or a punching bag to work up and dispel a rage; doing volunteer work with the less fortunate; becoming forgiving of oneself; giving oneself love; changing goals by giving up the impossible dream; letting go one's expectations of others so you won't be disappointed; doing a specific job unusually well; cooking a new dish; doing things for other people; being decisive; avoiding the spread of oneself and one's efforts too thin; avoiding dependence on only one person; stopping working for recognition; getting plenty of rest.

I would like to add a further prescription for overcoming depression. Many depressions, as we have seen, evolve from relationships with frustrating people, in addition to losses, unreachable goals, and so forth. It is vitally important that you learn how to cope with them. That is the reason why the chapter on depression follows those on anger, loneliness, dependence, and making friends. In these cases you are depressed because you have not learned how to fight back or otherwise defend yourself. You may be suffering from the illusion that nice people don't strike back, and thus your rage has nowhere to go but inward. Your ignorance of the nature of life, and the number of hostile, destructive people around, may be compounded by the false belief that you will lose something of value which cannot be replaced if you show your anger. If this is the case, the best and only way of curing your depression is to learn how to express your anger at those who mistreat you. It is not dishonorable to be angry, but it *is* dishonorable to be a dependent coward. If you are guilty of this, go back one chapter to "Anger." If you are not guilty of violating "the ouch principle," then you may go forward one chapter to "Improved Self-Assertion."

13　Improved Self-Assertion

An appropriate subtitle for this chapter is "On Being Real." To be unable to assert yourself or to make effective decisions is to subtract from your real self. To let others impose their will on you or to make the kinds of decisions which do not implement your goals or satisfy your needs is to participate in self-destructiveness.

Whether one is self-assertive or compliant depends on one's view of the world and one's place in it (Piotrowski, "The Human Movement Response," in *Perceptanalysis,* Chapter 6). If you have been trained to consider your actions and feelings important, if the tasks assigned to you by parents, teachers or employers have been realistic, if you have been taught that some efforts may be followed by rewards, then you are likely to feel confident that you can influence others and meet your needs through your own actions. If, on the contrary, your wishes and feelings were disregarded, you were never permitted to win an argument with your parents, and you were encouraged to try to meet goals beyond your capacities, it is likely that you face life feeling that others are more potent than you. You are likely to feel inadequate and valueless and in moments of decision to react in a compliant or self-effacing way.

It is perfectly true that certain occasions demand an appropriate degree of compliance. One can think of employment, military service, emergencies, meeting the appropriate needs of others, and so on. What you and I will be working on is the chronic, compulsive state of reacting to others as though your needs are valueless and their will must prevail. If this is the case, you may be pushed around by arrogant waiters, sleep with people you despise, let your immature children rule you, hate yourself for giving in to your inefficient or bullying supervisor, be robbed by inefficient or thievish corporations, and so forth.

In addition, if you cannot make effective decisions you will probably select the wrong mate, pick a career that dooms you to mediocrity, let failure and poverty exhaust your efforts on foolish projects, damage or ruin your business, ruin projects in a way that jeopardizes your company and thus your career, etc. There is a vicious spiral consisting of poor work habits, feelings of failure, poor decision-making, ultimate hopelessness, and compliance. You can enter this merry-go-round at any point. Instead of, as in the Spiritual, every rung going higher and higher, here each rung proceeds lower and lower.

How do you know that you are unnecessarily passive? There are a number of common indicators. Do you find yourself in situations which you had sworn that you would avoid? Are you frequently in the company of people whom you dislike? Do you take less responsible positions because you fear responsibility? Do you express yourself, your feelings, your actions, your mode of dress, your mannerisms according to your environment? Then you are not even just passive; you are a chameleon in sheep's clothing! Perhaps you are in a social situation and you find that you spend more than you want, bet more than you can afford, drink more than you can hold, stay up late until you ruin your capacity to function and enjoy the next day, have more sex than pleases you, eat to mollify your mother or hostess. You are passive and probably a coward to a considerable extent. We shall see some of the causes of your passivity and offer some pointers on how to overcome it. However, only *you* can cure your lifelong cowardice and self-blame.

What are some of the causes of pathetically reduced self-assertion? Yes, there are times when you are pathetic. Don't deny it. Just change. But, as in most sources of emotional discomfort, it is necessary to recognize the pathological influences which you are carrying forth into adulthood. Then exercise some self-discipline in order to substitute rewarding experiences for the degradation that you inflict on yourself through excessive compliance and other related forms of self-destructiveness.

The first basis of passivity to consider is *not knowing what you want or who you are.* Should this be your case, then you must either let others' preferences and desires rule the day, or assert yourself in an arbitrary, non-meaningful way. In the latter case you are likely to appear stupid or capricious. Therefore, the first step toward intelligent self-assertion and decision-making is *understanding your particular needs and the life style with which you are comfortable and which you find fulfilling.* This is important at many critical points in your life, and thus is worth repeating.

It is useful to try to see the relationship between your deep-felt *needs*, particularly those in which you feel frustrated, your *values* —i.e., those external circumstances, beliefs, and activities which you wish to continue and augment—and your *goals*, the condition in the future you wish to attain. Self-assertion and also proper decision-making then represent a healthy pattern of behaving. Starting with your feelings of dissatisfaction, or a knowledge of what pleases you or is valuable to you, you then plan your activities in such a way as to meet your needs and obtain pleasure according to your values.

Another source of passivity is excessive *dependency.* If you are dependent on other people in general, or on a particular individual, then you dare not antagonize people. To meet your childish needs, you then sacrifice more mature needs, ego, and a feeling of independence. You may think that you are concealing a tendency to cling to the other party, but the odds are that he/she knows your weaknesses and is playing them for all that they are worth. By being too weak to fetch for yourself you lay yourself open to bullying and a variety of kinds of deprivation since you cannot say "I want something and it is very important for me to get it." To overcome this cause of compliance it is necessary only to *grow up*. It is necessary to recognize that an adult leaves the nest and does not need parental figures to take care of basic needs. Rather, *an adult provides for his own necessities* if he lives alone, or shares responsibilities on an equal basis if he is part of a household. When you have reached this status, you can assert yourself because then another person cannot punish you by depriving you of something that you are already doing for yourself.

A closely related contributor to excessive passivity is *fear of loneliness*. Some people deny themselves their own reality because they feel that they will be rejected unless they let the other person do what he wants. Since there are plenty of selfish, uncaring individuals around, these pathetic dependent figures become prey to exploitation, get pushed around, and are deprived of enjoyable experiences in order not to be alone. Should you fall into this class, you must train yourself to believe that to be alone may be undesirable and even painful, but it is no disaster. You must discipline yourself to associate with people who will compromise with you and/or respect your wishes. You must develop techniques of meeting congenial people. Most important of all, *you must find ways of enjoying yourself while depending on your own resources.*

Guilt feeling contributes to passivity. Should you suffer from this malignant condition, then you will be unable to state your case. As a worthless person *you are entitled to bupkis* ("nothing" to those uninitiated in the Jewish tradition). As a wrongdoer, a sinner, a violater of all that is sacred, you are lucky that the rest of us virtuous creatures even let you survive. Of course, should there be reasonable grounds for you to feel guilty, it is self-destructive not to pay the penalty and try to make amends. It is better to do this than let your life be blighted by feelings of sin. To alleviate this condition may require psychotherapy, but in general

some *common sense evaluation of your responsibility is indicated.*
I have a patient who went through life in her mid-thirties feeling
guilty for the death of her mother when she was an infant. When
she was required to undergo major surgery, she felt impelled to
announce (no doubt to the astonishment of the surgical team) that
she was being punished for her guilt in this tragedy. This is an
example of neurotic feelings of guilt which are fostered by stupid
parents or devised by our defective brain to account for traumatic
circumstances beyond our control.

Fear of antagonizing others is a prime source of compliance.
What is often the case here is that the individual has developed
profound feelings of anger. Sometimes we either know or imagine we are so angry that we must fear our own destructiveness.
The child who is angry with a parent may assume the blame if the
parent should separate from the household or die or have an
accident. Then the individual develops magical thinking—i.e., the
belief that his anger is so strong that it can destroy others. To avoid
this possibility, he no longer asserts himself because of the *confu-
sion of anger with action.* It is much safer to do nothing, or to let
others take charge, because then the risk of destroying or antagonizing is less. Again, the answer is to know yourself well, to compensate for irrational feelings of anger, and to make decisions
which respect both your own needs and those of others with
whom you are related.

Feelings of failure can rob you of self-assertion. How can you
take a risk if your history has taught you that you will fail and thus
be scorned? This is a complicated matter, since failure can result
from a variety of causes. The feeling of being a failure or of being
inadequate can be ingrained from childhood. People with such
feelings experience themselves as washouts no matter what their
objective success. Indeed, they may even be effective decision-
makers but cannot enjoy the rewards of their labors because they
perceive the products and their very person to be inadequate.
They feel so inadequate that other people's wants are more important than their own. However, other people are failures, or con-

sider themselves to be so, for reasons occurring in their adult life. Perhaps the *standards set for them by their mates are unrealistic.* If so, *they should set their own standards.* They may be *in competition with more talented or older relatives.* The answer here is *to work for yourself* (to quote Willard and Margaret Beecher). You must live your own life and you must meet your own needs. Finally, some failure results because *the goals you have set for yourself are unrealistic.* You must *know your aptitudes and personality and either develop them further or work within your present limits.* More of this in Chapter 19 on effective decision-making.

Finally, realize that *some failures are "honorable."* Some individuals have worked hard, have developed their talents through self-sacrifice, but are unemployed momentarily or have failed for reasons beyond their control. It is part of life. When the recession hit the country, surely many of the millions of unemployed were loyal and efficient workers. Surely a capricious termination of a government grant or position or some natural disaster can keep a task from being accomplished. Failure is not sweet, but it need not be everlastingly bitter either.

Fear of failure is often associated with a degree of oversensitivity, with a feeling of vulnerability, with low self-esteem. Thus, one who suffers from this will *take no risks* and will *assume no responsibility.* The activities one performs, the tasks one suggests or volunteers for, the people one associates with are those which are simplest and familiar. How does a vulnerable person meet new friends or better lovers? How can he say this process or procedure will make our work more profitable, enjoyable, or efficient? How can he say that he'd rather go to a concert than to a ball game (or the reverse)? This worm can't, and until he can take risks he will serve as bait on somebody else's hook.

Another robber of self-assertion is *economic fear.* If you think that you and your family are inches from welfare or the soup line, then you had better listen very carefully to that creep who hired you. After all, who are you to deprive your children of that expensive summer camp, your wife of that mink coat which makes her friends hate her, those diamonds which she's scared to wear in public, etc.? Maybe that precious self-image of yours requires a Cadillac or another new car every year. You're going to a resort, and only the best accommodations will do? Well, stupid, the real cost of this is your economic fear and the necessity of making professional decisions on the basis of your employer's needs and not your own. *It is vital to develop a nest egg.* In this way, you can be yourself on the job and off it.

False ideologies also keep a person from defending his rights. One man told me of his inability to shut off a monopolizer in class. Since he was "taught to be polite" he could not risk losing his teacher's good opinion by expressing his feeling concerning the behavior of the other student. *It is often necessary to express your needs in a firm but non-abusive way.* Recently, when somebody left a transistor radio blaring unattended on a beach, I went and reduced the volume. When somebody who was engaged in a conversation some distance away objected, I told the guy that we were annoyed.

Transference from other situations can ruin your self-assertion. A too-powerful father or mother, or perhaps religious or educational mentors, can create in you a tendency to be compliant when you come into contact with others who superficially share the same characteristics. This is an example of what I called earlier overgeneralization. Fear or incapacity to deal with particular classes of people—e.g., one or the other sex, authority figures, those with particular heights or qualities of voice—should alert you to the fact that you are *transferring compliant reactions to the present from your childhood.* You can become more self-assertive by living in the present and dealing with the so-called authority figure according to your contemporary necessities. A particular hazard of transferring from childhood is that inappropriate anger or dependency is involved which affects the quality of the present personal relationship and ruins it because of projections and unreal expectations.

It is necessary to *distinguish between self-assertion and aggres-*

sion. The boundary involves the amount of hostility and respect for the other person's feelings and needs. While there are many situations in which one can prevail over the other person—for example, in dealing with strangers—it is self-destructive to attempt this in close dealings with friends, family, and so on. As one person put it: "Trying to lord it over people makes me unhappy. I don't get any satisfaction. You corner yourself. You've got to think there is somebody to lord it over you. I've cut whole segments out of my life by not thinking what people have in common."

It is not dishonorable to exchange feelings, to determine what the other person wants and holds valuable, and then to compromise. Should your offers to compromise be rejected, after you have expressed your needs, then you know the nature of your adversary and it might become necessary to be more firm or break off.

Another area requiring clarification is the distinction between *real and unreal obligations.* Certainly one of the characteristics of the decent person is that he/she fulfills his responsibilities. However, there are some responsibilities that are assumed voluntarily —for example, marriage and employment—and those that are involuntary. Nobody chooses his parents, and nobody wants a parent to be emotionally or economically dependent. The wise breadwinner is pleased to provide decently for his family, but is he under the obligation to ruin his health and peace of mind to give them luxuries? Some obligations are assumed because we are trained to feel guilty if we do not fulfill them. We are bad children, employees, mates. However, *our first obligation is to ourself.* I remember being accepted as a candidate for training at a well-known psychoanalytic institution. When I tried to make out a schedule to accommodate my previous commitments and necessities, I was told "Your first responsibility is to the——Center." My reaction was that if my first responsibility wasn't to myself, then it was to the Veterans Administration, which at the time was paying me a salary, while these authoritarian characters were offering me only the opportunity to obtain about $2,100 worth of tuition in exchange for about $5,000 of my time at the rate they would bill their clients. I recall getting really uptight, until I decided not to attend. When I called to state that I wasn't coming, I had a profound feeling of relief.

In evaluating what your obligations are, first determine what your personal necessities are. This ought to include what you must do for others who experience a commitment from you that will raise your sense of self-esteem. Then try to determine whether the other people can do something for themselves. If they can, insist that they contribute to their own welfare. Tolerate their pain; it won't hurt you a bit. Finally, in some cases, it may be necessary to call on others to assume their obligations. I have known cases of people who took exclusive care of aged parents and let well-to-do or capable brothers and sisters get away with selfish behavior. If an excessive burden descends on you, at least express your feelings and get rid of your selfish relatives. Finally, be careful in what you take from others. Why become obligated unnecessarily when you can avoid this through some self-restraint and independence?

To become more self-assertive, remember this: Self-respect will be yours if you reduce compliance and express your needs and wishes in a positive way.

14 *Changing Sexual Roles*

My discussion of sexual common sense has been placed toward the end of the book and allocated four chapters because it is genuinely a complex subject. It is difficult to have a happy sexual life while one is experiencing conflicts of values, various emotional discomforts, or frustration of basic needs. Sex is the vehicle of additional basic feelings such as anger and dependency. It is buffeted by early and current experiences as well as anxieties about the future. With some people, sexual behavior is determined by their life style. With others, the life style is determined by the peculiarities of their sexual drive.

It will be useful to begin our discussion with the question: What are male and female? The answer is incredibly complex. Sex can be defined from the histological, anatomical, physiological, biochemical, subjective, psychological, social, and legal points of view, and, no doubt, some others. Let me alert you to the fact that individuals who seem to be clearly of one sex by a particular criterion may be clearly of the other sex by different criteria! By becoming aware of the complexity of sexual behavior, anatomy, and physiology, you will be more tolerant of your weaknesses and, one hopes, of those of your partner(s). Moreover, by understanding that sex is not "created" by any single factor and that there are multiple influences on your behavior and experiences, you will become more open to trying new styles of relating. Only if sex is fixed once and for all can it be justified that there is only one way to do it and let it become a part of your life. To repeat, sexual behavior, feelings, and attitudes are shaped by multiple causes in a complex series of internal and external events. At any given time, sexual responsiveness is shaped by attitudes from other areas, the nature of one's mate, life style, and so forth. Finally, one's sexual attitudes influence other people so that a cycle is set up between our sexual behavior and how others relate to us, which in turn reinforces or changes the original behavior.

I find it useful to think of sex as having many dimensions, as a solid object has the dimensions of height, width, breadth, weight, and center of gravity—for analogy a container of gas that involves pressure, volume, temperature, with changes in one component affecting the others. The dimensions that define masculinity and femininity are:

1. *Chromosomal.* There are characteristic differences in the chromosomes and other cellular structures (the histology) of males and females. Furthermore, there are particular diseases and other well-known abnormalities that are associated with defects in the sex chromosomes, or with abnormal numbers or absences of particular chromosomes.

2. *Anatomical.* The obvious differences between the external and internal genitalia of males and females is really not so obvious. Hormonal deficiencies and surpluses at different times of development (from the fetal stage on) can change or conceal the basic sexual anatomical characteristics of the external or internal genitalia.

3. *Biochemical.* The characteristic male and female sex hormones are secreted by both sexes although generally in different amounts. Furthermore, one of the hormones vital to sexual development isn't even secreted by the gonads. Androsterone, which changes the somewhat neutrally shaped fetus to the male shape and virilizes women who receive it through prescription or

through disease processes, is secreted not by the testes but by the covering (cortex) of the adrenal gland.

4. *Physiological.* There are sexual differences in susceptibility to disease and mortality (more males die at any particular age), and even at birth males and females show differences in sensitivity and skin conductance.

5. *Subjective.* One's *gender* or identification with one sex or the other begins to be fixed at birth. Some hospitals have the custom of placing male infants in blue blankets and female in pink ones. This is generally determined by the appearance of the external genitalia, although this is by no means a perfect indicator of chromosomal, biochemical, or internal anatomical sex. Beyond early childhood, when sex typing is firmly imprinted, it becomes very difficult for a person to change his feeling of identification with one or the other sex so that emotional problems must be considered when medical studies indicate that the person's basic sex was misjudged at birth.

6. *Psychological.* There are well-established differences in the *average* personality, stamina, approach to intellectual problems, interests, values, and so forth between males and females from youth on. Of course, there is a great deal of overlapping. These differences are probably partially inherited and partially cultural. Anyway, if it's news to you, men and women think differently.

7. *Social.* The culture of this and every country generally pressures males and females to act differently if they are to receive rewards, be socially acceptable, and find some niche. Be forewarned, however, that in every culture there are a large number of subcultures, and the favored behaviors may differ considerably in each group.

8. *Legal.* There are different requirements for each sex that are determined by law in the areas of marriage, military service, jury duty, and so forth.

One of the most consequential social questions of our time is whether there are changing attitudes and thus changing roles and relationships between the sexes. This is pointed up by such a

newspaper headline as: "COURT AWARDS CHILD TO LESBIAN."
This item points out the veracity of the French saying, "The more
things change, the more they remain the same." Obviously, lesbian sexual orientation has been with us at least since the classical
Greek period. Perhaps what is occurring is a greater degree of
openness in expressing basic trends which deviate from some
stereotyped, moralistic norm. As more individuals express openly
their rights to deviate (even openly), they become more aware of
each other and band together to obtain support and achieve what
they consider to be their civil right of sexual expression. I would
like to say parenthetically at this point that I believe that *consent-
ing adults* should be able to do what they please privately, but
emotional common sense dictates that sexual deviations not be
propagandized toward developing children and adolescents.
Some youth can be swayed in their sexual development because
of experiential and perhaps biological influences. They would pay
too high a price of misery and rejection to allow them to be seduced for the momentary pleasure of an adult whose sexual practices are deviant from the norm of the majority of the community.
It is probably true that some people are imprinted with a tendency to seek homosexual partners by very early hormonal or
environmental conditions. However, this need not be the case
with all potential homosexuals. Therefore, it is socially desirable
that homosexual adults not be permitted to seduce youth who
otherwise would develop a more socially acceptable means of
sexual expression.

There is now a greater degree of openness concerning the discussion of sexual practices than in the past, and it is possible that
certain patterns are quite innovative for American society. In
addition to members of male and female "Gay Liberation" (are
they really so gay?), many other individuals deliberately refuse the
status of marriage. Indeed, there are today many women who
choose to have children without being tied legally or emotionally
to a husband. This is a downright selfish attitude that risks an
emotionally incomplete upbringing for the children and the likeli-

hood of their becoming deprived, demanding adults.

It is a legitimate decision to make if one decides not to marry. The reasons might be perhaps either fear of closeness or the belief that other values such as one's career or need for excitement would make one an unsatisfactory mate. Perhaps such a person cannot relate well on an intimate basis. Such a decision, which conceivably ought to be reviewed periodically, need not be final. One cannot predict what events or self-knowledge will occur to change one's view of life or bring need for warmth and contact to the fore. The person who *is* interested in marriage, however, ought to be aware that today's modern world permits many individuals to take the alternative option. Therefore, emotional common sense dictates that you exchange feelings with any person whom you may feel is a potential mate. If your own need to marry is pressing, which by itself deserves self-exploration, then you should determine the relevant attitudes of your intended. There is a tactful way to explore his/her ideas concerning his own future, without implying that you will interpret this to be a commitment.

A closely related problem results from the high rate of divorce and separation. This is probably due to the ridiculous social pressure for youngsters to marry before they are mature, self-aware, or economically self-sufficient. Nevertheless, large numbers of individuals find themselves in the middle of their life unexpectedly without a mate. Frequently their state of mind is angry, frustrated, economically concerned, and defensive. It is possible that as the individual and his/her mate lived together, one or both of them developed in ways that could not be predicted at the time of marriage, or one of them matured and the other stagnated or regressed (e.g., into alcoholism, mental illness, overdependency). In any event, the person finds himself seeking companionship with perhaps not much more self-awareness than when he began his marriage. I deliberately used the term *companionship* because it is ambiguous. Individuals react differently to the breakup of an intense meaningful relationship. Some avoid people, others need contact but cannot stand sex; still others want sex but can't stand commitment, and some immediately want to remarry.

It is useful to explore why the breakup of an important relationship occurred. There is an overwhelming tendency to blame the other person. At the minimum, however, you either encouraged or permitted that relationship. There was likely some blind spot, some lack of self- or social understanding which prevented you from understanding your needs or those of the other person. It is also likely that *you were active* in spoiling the relationship. You must explore what you did to provoke the other person's anger or dissatisfaction. I find that when people complain about a particular characteristic in another person, they are likely to show this themselves. This tendency is described as *hostile identification with pain-inflicting parents.* Thus, explore your own part in any difficult relationships in which you play a role. If need be, enter psychotherapy, because this is potentially a means of more rapidly achieving better self-understanding and more compatible social relationships.

Another important social change is the relatively large number of people who express a preference for multiple relationships over exclusive ones. I don't doubt that in every age such people existed. They probably won't admit it, but it may well be a result of some problem in achieving closeness rather than a closely reasoned decision. Anyway, when I was a youth in the forties it was certainly "the thing" to have a girl and to get married ultimately. Ditto for the ladies. The period of searching, experimenting and generally raising hell was regarded as *delightful* but temporary by the guys and *disgusting* but temporary by the gals. Today, things are different. There are many people who prefer as a life style to enter into multiple sexual relationships at a particular stage of their life. From their point of view, they get one kind of jollies from one person, a second kind from somebody else, and so forth. By not committing themselves to one person they are spared obligations, responsibilities, demands. Multiple relationships are also a security mechanism, "guaranteeing" some contact. One man asked: "Who is going to hold my hand when I'm married?" To this man, even a marriage is no guarantee of his emotional security, and other partners are needed to meet his cravings. Emotional common sense dictates that if you are interested in a meaningful relation-ship you interview, screen, analyze, or in any other way determine the nature of the beast so that you are not deceived, seduced into one-night stands, or used for the trivial gratification of others. Conversely, if one's life style is against emotional commitment to one person, it is equally emotional common sense for him to make his intentions known clearly. Should this apply to you, you might object that you will not be able to obtain companionship and sexual gratification by exposing your intentions. That is true, but you will also avoid guilt feelings, scenes, unanticipated demands, promises, and other avoidable and uncomfortable situations which will unnecessarily damage your self-esteem.

One of the healthiest changes in sexual matters is the liberation of women. Incredibly, it was denied by the so-called educated classes at one time that women had any sexual desires. After that, while it was acknowledged that women enjoyed "it," they were ruined if they handled it injudiciously before marriage. Now the pendulum has gone to the other extreme. For example, a physi-cian told me of an adolescent girl who came in to be fitted for a diaphragm before taking a trip to Europe alone. When the doctor called her mother, she replied that it was better that the girl be protected than come home pregnant. This is basically highly per-missive, since in times past many young girls were unsupervised and yet were able to deny themselves. What has changed is the spirit of the times. Sexual freedom is widely encouraged in all ways for those who are so inclined. It will take a generation or two to determine whether the participants in this new culture, and their children, will be less neurotic and better related than those of my own uptight generation.

Another healthy change is the more accepting attitude toward masturbation. As a boy I remember sneaking glances at a sex manual which seriously stated that tuberculosis and other dread diseases were the result of "self-abuse." Today, instead of this being a hidden (though universal) practice, it is discussed openly by people as a suitable release when they do not have a sexual partner. As an older person put it, "The most gratifying thing is when you find somebody else who does it too."

It will be useful to explore whether men and women have different values. In my Participation/Discussion groups any general statement is an invitation to a fight. For example, should somebody say, "All men . . ." or "Women tend to . . ." there is sure to be somebody whose experience is different. Therefore, although I believe that there are larger numbers of men or women who behave in particular ways, or have particular values, in practice it is important to understand the motives of the particular individual with whom you are relating. A characteristic stereotyped statement might be that women are more interested in security while men are more interested in conquest. This is a typically meaningless statement. Security means marriage to some people and celibacy or multiple relationships to others. Similarly, there are many women who count the number of their sexual experiences as men have traditionally kept track of their own. I was informed that I was No. 17 for the first woman I had sex with.

It would be ridiculous to ignore anatomy. It is true that on the average men are taller and stronger than women, and only women can give birth. Since in our culture most men and women accept the idea that if anyone is to take care of an infant it will be the woman, then various implications follow. As long as the infant requires close attention, the man will work and the woman will be the housekeeper. Sometimes these roles have been reversed.

Any person who enjoys the idea of having children must explore the attitude of his potential partner toward children and the rearing of them. Things being as they are, a woman is more likely to require the security of a man who will permit her to raise children and is more likely to anticipate with pleasure the role of the parent. Giving birth is an intense experience which only the woman has. She literally creates the child and thus is prone to feel closer to her children, at least initially. This is one basis for the plaint of so many women that men don't want to settle down. From the point of view of some males, marriage and parenthood imply increased obligations which are more beneficial for the woman than the man. However, this feeling is by no means universal. I know one man who married a girl he had known for two weeks, impregnated her, got a pipe and a dog and believed his needs to be fulfilled. Conversely, there are some women who value their careers and feel no loss at not being married.

Because of the biological/cultural tendency of so many women to prefer the married/parental state, they have not trained themselves to think as independent human beings. They require a man to impregnate them and then to go out and work to maintain the nest. Some of them are basically dependent. This lack of training in being independent and competent creates a generalized need for a man to take charge and to be emotionally giving. To relate to such a woman is to feel swallowed up by her dependency. Thus, it makes sense to train little girls to relate to the real world of affairs and then hope that they will marry because of love for a particular man and as an improvement on their life rather than to fill basically immature cravings. Commitment ought to be given as the expression of respect and exchange, not to meet the clutching of an insecure person who can't fetch for herself (or himself).

Most men and women are trained to take different roles. The pattern described here is often followed, though to a lesser extent than previously, by the younger people today. It has been customary for the man to take the initiative in meeting a woman at a social event, and subsequently to contact her to make a date, to pay for the expenses of the evening, and finally to escort the woman home. Then there may be a struggle on the couch, initiated by the man, and resisted with different degrees of intensity and sincerity by the woman. This procedure is self-destructive for women. After all, they have eyes and can detect those men who turn them on. They have telephones and can make their own arrangements to meet their sexual and other emotional needs.

Today, they have enough money to pay their way separately or even with a date into a movie. And they have voices to indicate clearly their sexual desire or wish for abstinence.

The result of the present system is to make women feel as though they are sexually exploited, economically prostituting themselves, and the passive victims of hordes of rampant men whose only wish is to "enjoy their bodies." This is largely correct. With the influx of young people into the metropolitan centers, there is such a cornucopia of sexually eligible people, entertainment, parties, etc., that it is genuinely easier for a man to go from bed to bed than to commit himself to the problems of establishing a firm relationship. Of course, many women experience life in the same way.

Men and women tend to take an adversary attitude toward each other; they try to exploit the other, defend their own ego, play it cool and not be too committed, appearing plastic to meet the assumed needs of the other, giving false impressions, etc. How does one defend oneself against this pathological social condition? The first task is to recognize and avoid sexual games. This we will discuss in the next chapter. Then, it is important to develop one's personality and resources in order to attract a better sort of suitor and to be strong enough for the long haul. This will be discussed in Chapter 16.

15 *Sexual Self-Destructiveness*

Much of sexual self-destructiveness is perpetrated through initiating or being the victim of sexual games. I define a sexual game as an attempt to deceive the other person or oneself concerning one's real feelings and/or intentions through misleading or ambiguous words and actions. Since sex is potentially the most intense pleasure of life, this state of affairs seems to be ridiculous. Why should it be necessary for people who desire each other sexually to have to manipulate each other into a sexual relationship? The reason is very simple. Not only do individuals often act in their worst interests, but sex is also the carrier of feelings toward parents, self, society, and so forth. When you go to bed with somebody there is an entire cast of characters in addition to the heroine and hero.

The nature of the seeming conflict between the sexes can be illustrated by these direct quotes:

He: "The average unwed male would be doomed to celibacy if he didn't pretend a little bit."

She: "I want to get to know him as a person before we have sex."

Obviously, as long as there is the demand to get to know somebody, one has to run the risk that the data offered is tainted with selfish self-interest.

There are many purposes to sexual games, and several of them may be functioning simultaneously. Since most sexual games are the result of neurotic goals, distortions of reality, inability to relate, or psychopathic exploitation, one can easily see that to initiate them is to engage in self-destructiveness in one's personal life. Furthermore, it is vital to recognize these games so that one is not the victim of another person's destructiveness.

Some of the many goals of sexual games are listed here:

1. *Reducing vulnerability.* To ensure one's emotional safety—that is, to avoid being hurt, rejected, or found inadequate—many people engage in amounts or patterns of sexuality which they would prefer not to. They relate sexually immediately or not at all, or yield to sexual practices they dislike, to avoid having any confrontation that will reduce their feelings of self-esteem.

2. *Avoiding commitment.* At a given time, one may feel anxious at the idea of having a committed, exclusive relationship. Therefore his sexual behavior will be designed to keep his partner off balance and not expect a continuing relationship.

3. *Setting up obligations.* To demonstrate the plasticity of sexual behavior and how it can be molded to meet quite extraneous considerations, we list this kind of manipulation next to avoiding commitment. To some women, the suggestion of sex becomes tantamount to a discussion of marriage. The slightest penetration is the equivalent of marriage vows. To break these vows is to become the victim of a great campaign of guilt-provocation.

4. *Attempting to deceive.* There is about as much outright lying in sex as there is in business. Probably more, since the laws of the states influence business procedures, but sexual behavior is generally limited only by one's imagination and childhood upbringing. People lie in order to conceal their feelings about the other person and their intentions. The forms of lying include false statements, social pressure, use of money and surroundings, and being more or less sexual than your body signals. Sexual exploitation is used for marriage, money, business, social contacts, good times, entrée into particular circles, as well as just plain sex.

5. *Attempting to control.* Since so many people regard sex as the emotional equivalent of their pay check, they are subject to manipulative attempts at control. I remember a lady who once kissed me good night and told me that was my ration for the evening. I told myself that when kisses were rationed it was a disaster economy I didn't want to be a part of. This sort of iniquity occurs within and without marriage, and women are generally the instigators. Nobody likes to feel that he must give this or that before he can have some sexual experience, so that the result is doubly self-destructive. First, the other person is resentful; secondly, you have deprived yourself of a good time.

6. *Inability to express feelings directly.* This is a serious problem when it occurs in the sexual area as in many others. Sometimes a relationship is not started because one person cannot tell the other person about the warmth he/she experiences. On the other hand, contacts can be continued indefinitely when no longer desired because "I don't want to hurt the other person's feelings." In either case, it is a game with the players losing.

7. *To bolster self-esteem.* Both men and women like to "score points." Lots of genital contact can become the means of assuaging parental criticism and teacher's lack of approval. Making orgasmic experience, or the lack of it, the way of compensating for the hurt feelings of twenty or more years before is only one more bit of evidence of the defectiveness of the human brain.

8. *For adventure.* Some people have a craving for excitement. The dullness of their lives causes them to want to step out on the town. It has no meaning except that it is more stimulating than the overall grayness of one's existence. Obviously, unless there is a partner with the same minimal commitment of feelings, someone will be disappointed.

9. *Avoidance of loneliness.* If you are the type of person for whom loneliness is the worst of experiences, then sexuality or even marriage with unloved or disliked partners is your probable fate.

10. *Customary rituals.* It is interesting that even in the privacy of personal relationships, people insist on following the requirements of convention. They take society to bed with them. It is expected that the man will try and the woman will resist. I have known women who spoke of their disappointment when the man didn't make a pass at them, even though they had no intention of having sex with him. Many men make their pitch as a matter of form, expecting neither acceptance nor ultimate satisfaction.

11. *Self-deception.* Sexual games are often entered into because the players cannot bear the thought of being unloved or unloving. They are open to any kind of lie in order to tell themselves that they are attractive. The lie may be verbal, or it may consist of concealing from oneself that the behavior of the other person is harsh, inconsiderate, unloving, and generally indifferent to one's welfare.

To help you recognize specific sexual games, to break out of this neurotic pattern, and to defeat the intentions of others, I have listed some of the games under emotionally related categories:

SECURITY

1. *Ambiguity.* For this you set up a smokescreen in order not to reveal your true intentions. It is not clear whether or not you want sex, relate it to marriage, are interested in just having a date or in continuing the relationship.

2. *Giving.* This involves trying to entrap the other person through a sense of obligation. Lend your car, make lavish dinners, spend lots of money, always listen to the tale of woe regardless of your mood, etc.

3. *Instant sex.* To make sure that the other person won't run away, take off your clothes immediately. The futility of guaranteeing the lover's presence is obvious. I think that handcuffs and knee irons are better, but they will require some fancy bodily contortions to enjoy sex.

DECEPTION

1. *Outright lying.* Both men and women are capable of total distortions of their intentions, backgrounds, finances, and everything else important in order to obtain or avert the possibility of sexual relations. There is no guarantee that you won't be taken in. If in doubt ask questions. If you are deceived, refuse to see the person again. A liar will damage you in more ways than sexual deceit.

2. *Going out with an impossible person.* Some people will form temporary relationships for self-convenience. They know quite well that they will never marry or form a deep relationship with their partner for reasons of age, religion, finances, appearance, and so on. They will cheerfully permit the other person to develop deep feelings based on false appearances so that they will temporarily have a partner, either until their circumstances improve or until somebody better comes along. The only defense for the patsy is to try to get the other person to express himself as clearly as possible. Ask questions, stop talking, and listen. Yes, I said stop talking. Shut your mouth and listen. If your lover is closemouthed, he/she may have a reason for not giving himself away.

3. *Pretending to have feelings.* This little game is meant to preserve one's own ego, not necessarily to damage the other person. I have a patient who for a period of ten months did not reveal to her lover that she wasn't having an orgasm. The problem of stating this is harder late than soon. This kind of behavior is obviously designed to keep a weak relationship going for fear that it will collapse when the partner realizes that there are limits to his lover's responsiveness.

4. *Playing a false role.* Individuals pretend to be stronger or weaker than they are in order to entice the other person, or give the kind of impression they think is desired. I know of one woman who often took the initiative in a relationship until it came to paying the bill. In this kind of situation some men are likely to pay for only their own share and then walk out. To play the role of

being strong is particularly self-destructive. The other person becomes far too dependent. Then, when your own feelings of weakness require you to stop giving, or, God forbid, even ask for help, you are met with expressions of disbelief and even rage. "I thought you were so strong."

TRANSFERENCE

1. *Attributing false positive qualities.* Sometimes we expect that a person with trivial similarities to our parents will continue to treat us in the same way as our parents did when we were children. A partner like the strong father or warm mother is a good example. Unfortunately, the partner may have similar expectations of exceptional treatment, and that's where the conflict and frustration begin.

2. *Attributing false negative qualities.* We can just as easily exaggerate the meaning of various unpleasant qualities because they are reminiscent of how somebody else treated us. A woman once said to me, after I had spent a quiet Saturday evening with some friends in her company after an exhausting six-day week, "You are just like my ex-husband. He always was passive." She K.O.'d herself.

3. *Falling in love with cold, indifferent people.* This is an attempt to obtain vindication for childhood feelings of rejection. We select somebody with some slight resemblance to our parents, somebody who very likely has no warm feelings for us. Then, because of their very coldness, we try to make them love us just as we would have wanted our parents to love us.

CHILDHOOD FANTASIES

1. *Brunnhilde.* Some children have exaggerated feelings about their own worth. When they grow up they expect their mate to prove himself/herself just as the Norse hero Siegfried had to go through the magic fire in order to rescue Brunnhilde.

2. *Sleeping Beauty.* A closely related fantasy is the need to be recognized as exceptionally valuable, even, for example, as the prince was able to see the virtues of the Sleeping Beauty while she was asleep.

3. *The Princess.* This is a form of sexual game in which the player, not always a woman, demands special treatment in return for sexuality. The gift of one's body on an exclusive, legal basis is considered to be so great that the recipient is considered to be obligated on a lifelong basis to revere, spoil, and behave on a subordinate basis.

4. *Don Juan.* Although named after a gentleman, this form of self-destructiveness is not exclusively male. The basic fantasy is that there is a partner who can satisfy all of one's needs. As a result, there is no tolerance for the frailties of one's sexual partner. The experience of imperfection or lack of total gratification leads to the immediate severing of the relationship and the quest for someone new who will not be disappointing.

5. *Rebelliousness.* Selecting a partner of whom parents would disapprove. This is a terribly poor way of selecting a mate. It implies that one's values are significantly different from those of one's parents. Unfortunately, the mate frequently turns out to be a carbon copy of one parent. If the partner is actually significantly different from the parents, you may then find that you have not rejected your parental household as much as you think.

CONFLICT

1. *Sado-masochism.* This is a very complicated life style between two partners in which one plays the role of aggressor while the other plays victim. It frequently evolves from ill-treatment when one was young, fantasies of revenge and of having a really good parent, and liberal quantities of self-deception as to how it really was.

Games and other sexually self-destructive behavior are frequently exceptionally difficult to change. The reason is partially the amount of short-term gratification obtained from sex. The psychologists who have studied how people learn state that behavior which accompanied some pleasure is likely to be repeated. As a result, self-destructive sexual behavior will also be repeated even if it violates emotional common sense. By this I specifically mean that sexual attitudes that are hurtful to one's partner, or are counterproductive in achieving one's own valued life style, are reluctantly given up regardless of their results.

How, then, can you change your sexual attitudes and behavior? Part of the solution is to have a clear alternative. Then, as you are confronted with choices and decisions, you can ask yourself whether the results will be consistent with some larger life plan. It is likely that there will be deviations from plan, but if you have confidence that you want to change and resolutely refuse to add to your emotional discomfort in the form of doubt caused by self-directed accusations of guilt, then you will be able to improve your life style.

In addition to self-destructive sexual games, there are harmful patterns which make living with a particular person a miserable experience. Check yourself out to see if you make any of these mistakes.

MISTAKES MAKING MATES MISERABLE

1. *Nagging.* Learn to take no for an answer. In some states it is legal to assault nags physically. They deserve it.

2. *Abusiveness.* To curse and emphasize the weaknesses and faults of a mate, or to exaggerate criticism in any way, is to destroy the other partner's good feelings for you. Abuse is often remembered longer than kind words.

3. *Permitting mistreatment.* By letting yourself be abused, exploited, or otherwise mistreated, you ruin your own good spirits, set a poor model for your children, and make your mate feel guilty.

He will then continue to abuse you until you stop him by punishing him. Stop the vicious circle immediately. Call the police if necessary.

4. *Possessiveness.* If you are overly controlling and stifle your partner, you will end up married to an uninteresting, sniveling, resentful dishrag. Then, when you complain to your buddies or the bridge club about what an uninteresting, passive, dependent mate you have, the only honest answer will be that you created your own dissatisfaction.

5. *Living through the other party.* Do your own thing. Then if your partner fails, it is his failure and you can reassure him. The last thing you want to do is to attack somebody for failing or for slowing down, feeling that it becomes your personal failure. This is the road to being hated.

6. *Demanding that the partner match our ideals.* You are probably sufficiently confused to have difficulty running your own affairs with emotional common sense. Where do you get off setting standards for other people?

7. *Showing passiveness and evading responsibility.* To let your resources atrophy and to be reliant excessively on the other party is to reduce the quality of your own life because then only one brain and pair of hands are at work. It is also an invitation to be treated with contempt and to be ignored when decisions are made.

8. *Excessive ties with parents.* Nobody knows better than you how you were mistreated when you were at home and the problems your parents had in running their lives with rationality and compassion toward each other. To insist that they be taken into consideration in the decision-making now only means that you are still an obedient child. Make you own mistakes.

9. *Using sex as reward and punishment.* Sex should not be contingent on the good behavior of your partner. The central nervous system does not react kindly to having sexual experiences associated with conflicts, anger, and frustration. If you take your anger to bed you will also have as bed partners your lawyers, an

accountant, a judge, and a jury of twelve. Watching carefully will be your children, the neighbors, and your parents.

10. *Provoking a fight as a test of love.* This is a sign of a serious personality disturbance. Anybody who feels that only a loving person will fight with him is nuts. It shows that he lacks influence over the other person and cannot express his anger and love directly. You can certainly make a situation worse and lose your partner unexpectedly with this foolish tactic.

11. *Getting the last word.* There are more important issues in life than who is right or wrong. I have had the opportunity as a psychotherapist to hear about fights over such vital issues as when to put the butter away, whether cremation is a satisfactory way of disposing of a body, and so on. Express your feelings calmly, insist that the other person respect your right to have an opinion, then shut up. (Refer back to #1, *Nagging.*)

12. *Competitiveness.* While we are in this area, do your own thing. Remember that when you are competitive with your partner it is somebody you love whom you are defeating.

13. *Interrupting.* Not to let the other person express his/her feelings or to finish a thought is highly irritating. It points to a lack of consideration of the other person's feelings and a dominating attitude. Have no doubts, you will be treated accordingly.

14. *Holding back your feelings.* As we have noted repeatedly, this affects your own spirits and must have a deleterious effect on the relationship. Let the other person know of your love and your anger and your dependency. But do this in a way that the message can be heard.

15. *Expecting total satisfaction.* This is the royal road to unhappiness. It guarantees that you will be not only frustrated but will find it necessary to demand and intimidate others to get what you believe is coming to you. You will achieve not satisfaction but fury.

At this point I have reviewed many of the self-destructive ways in which people act—toward their mates, other members of their family, in business, and so on. I believe that through self-understanding and with some self-discipline, you can improve the quality of your life by following these guidelines.

If there are particular problem areas which you feel are beyond your own capacity to deal with, it would be self-destructive to suffer unnecessarily. You should then try to get psychotherapeutic assistance. Chapter 20 offers help in choosing a therapist.

In the next chapter I will discuss meaningful sexual relationships, I trust, without any of the pap you are accustomed to read. To expect sex to be something else than what it really is is to invite disillusionment.

16 *Achieving Meaningful Sexual Relationships*

The first step in achieving a meaningful sexual relationship is to clarify what sex may mean to you. It is my experience that there are few generalities which apply to human behavior, and one of them is that people differ. However, by understanding yourself better, you will be able to relate better to your partner and be a helpful parent, friend, lover, etc.

Sex is usually misestimated. When you are having it regularly it is devalued, and when you are not having it regularly, then it is overvalued. It is also the case that there are many individualized subjective meanings to sexual experience. In general, to have been raised by caring parents is to experience a need to continue some kind of close relationship. Thus, a consistent avoidance of close relationships points to some problem with intimacy. I know one man who for a period of time behaved promiscuously despite having a wife and children. One day he asked himself, "Why aren't I home?"

Perhaps the key question to ask oneself in determining the meaning of sexual experience is: How personal a relationship do I require? It is possible to be satisfied with almost any genital in a moment of loneliness or necessity. Impersonal sex has been described as being the equivalent of masturbation. It is also possible to focus upon the sexual aspect of a relationship in order to avoid other kinds of intimacy. Sex can be used to relieve tension, anger, anxiety, guilt, and other emotional discomforts. It can be a simple ego-enhancing "trip." Some claim that they have sex for "medical reasons," others in order to be compassionate. "Oh, you poor thing. You don't have a man. Let me help you." I know of one woman who will have sex only if the man loves her, but she does not require herself to love the man! Sex can also be part of a companionable relationship that is meaningful and pleasurable but without great commitment between the partners.

For still others there is a quality about sexual experience which is deeply spiritual, perhaps even mystical. It is emotionally impossible for them to have a sexual relationship without deep knowledge of, and commitment from, the other person. They may live their entire lifetime without having more than one sexual partner. Should their mate die, then they may not experience the emotional possibility of forming a new relationship if nobody appears who can re-establish feelings like those with the first partner. This may be expressed something like this: "I want to feel that I really want to be there with him (her)."

Now, since attitudes toward sex vary between people, it may be self-destructive to assume that your partner shares your values. Thus, in the process of forming a new relationship, or in taking stock of one that you now have, it is useful to exchange feelings to see what compromises may be needed, or whether the continuance of the relationship is indeed feasible. It is particularly important, in order to avoid conflicts with friends and poor decisions for yourself, to be aware of the vast changes that can take place in a person's sexual life style. Bachelors do marry and father children, and some monogamous ladies do have multiple sexual relationships after a divorce.

If you should find yourself in a position which requires finding a sexual partner, what emotional common sense applies to your situation? Here are a few basics from the folklore of experience:

1. *Different people have a different pace with which they ap-*

proach a sexual experience. To be sexual too soon or too late may mean the termination of what might be a highly satisfactory relationship. One middle-aged woman who had not had any sex in the three years since her husband died, expressed her values in a discussion of sexual experiences by stating in an accusatory manner that "Isn't this what is meant by being a loose woman?" The writer could not repress the nastier side of his nature by commenting (as discussion leader) that to be "a loose woman was an orthopedic, not psychological, concept."

2. *You can't relate to everybody.* To strike out with one person does not mean that you are undesirable. If you consistently strike out, then it would be useful for you to take stock of your social attitudes.

3. *You must accept yourself as a person.* It is vital that you build up your ego so that you see yourself as being as worthwhile as anybody. To look for a mate and relate to one as a piece of garbage is to invite abuse or to avoid people who could care for you.

4. *Don't pursue somebody who is rejecting or indifferent.* In the words of George Wither:

> Great, or good, or kind, or fair,
> I will ne'er the more despair;
> If she love me, this believe,
> I will die ere she shall grieve;
> If she slight me when I woo,
> I can scorn and let her go;
> For if she be not for me,
> What care I for whom she be?

5. *Different people require different amounts of sex.* Reference to the Kinsey volumes on the sexual behavior of men and women will convince you of the vast differences in the capacities or sexual interest in any particular age group. There are even important religious differences in sexual expressiveness!

One of the things that modern people have to consider is whether to engage in "instant sex." The motive may be great emotional stress, as in the case of a nineteen-year-old girl who had sex for the first time immediately after her mother's funeral. It can occur because of loneliness: "Just being in bed with a body was better than nothing." Others comply to the request in order that the person "will love you."

I would like to approach this question from the point of view of people who seek a meaningful relationship but with respect for the different needs of people. The chief criterion ought to be whether it makes more or less likely the achievement of a good relationship. For some, instant sex is evidence of lack of caring. For others, it is evidence of caring or "being turned on." What affects feelings experienced after an immediate sexual experience is the degree of intimacy that is required by the individual. The case *for* instant sex is that it *may* make possible the knowledge as to whether the partner is sexually suitable. On the other hand, the capacity to enjoy and provide enjoyment fluctuates from time to time so that the sample provided may not be representative. Moreover, sex is inevitably at least a partially intimate experience. You can wake up with a partner with personality quirks far different from those you anticipated. A slower approach to sex would permit some warning that there are attitudes and habits which must be accommodated or which would prove disastrous to a relationship. If the shock of dissatisfaction can be avoided, then a firm relationship may take hold. However, with all of my doubts and red lights, instant sex will continue. A man told one of my groups: "In New York City you're lucky to get away without sex for a week."

What do people expect in a relationship? What don't people expect in a relationship? They expect romance, commitment, devotion, excitement, understanding, trustworthiness, and so on. Their expectations are both real and unreal.

Let us consider romance. As my colleague Jane Morrin asks, "Is there reality in romance?" Emotional common sense dictates that we remember that Romance is the name of a language; it defines also a strong expressive quality in music and is related to the

French name for fiction. One approaches romance starry-eyed. "We want the ideal, but we do not want to work in order to be the other person's ideal." Romance is certainly a deep, beautiful feeling. Sometimes it extends throughout a couple's life, and sometimes it doesn't last beyond the first date. Feelings of romance may be the illusion that childhood or adolescent fantasies of emotional beauty have come to pass. It can be the projection to a partner of the fantastic images we created for solace when we were unhappy adolescents. Emotional hunger can be the basis for self-deception. Somebody I know once commented, "in the consummation lies the destruction of the romance." It is not correct to say that "love is blind." Love, rather, creates images and feelings. Love, indeed, may be hallucinatory. Let me not be misinterpreted as being opposed to romance. I merely recognize that feelings between people change as they go through life together.

Commitment is a particular area of conflict. Just as some individuals are paralyzed by the idea, others require it prematurely. The key difference is between the person who feels inadequate and thus cannot maintain a close relationship, and the person who feels inadequate and therefore requires a close relationship. Perhaps the best approach is to see whether two people's life styles mesh and it is in their best interests to stay together. This is entirely different from feeling obligated because of verbal promises or coital thrusts.

How long is a commitment? Some people experience their marriage vows as being for life. I know a woman who was outraged because her marriage was about to end in divorce. Since she and her husband took vows in their early twenties, when they were in their forties (with a late adolescent, independent son) she felt that he was breaking his commitment. He was interested in other women, she mistrusted him financially, he permitted his mistress to alienate the affections of their son, but he should still keep his promise to remain married to her for life. The key issue here, of course, is the overestimation of the value of marriage. It is more important for her to be married to a shallow man than to have an honest separation and be available for a new relationship.

What about trustworthiness and reliability? Considering the demands that life places on people both as individuals and as couples, this is a key factor to be sought for and developed in one's own personality. I know one person who said that "I feel uptight if the other person isn't trustworthy." A young woman was so pleased at a distinguished man's courtship that she lent him five hundred dollars, and was infuriated to learn that not only wasn't he a surgeon but she didn't know his correct name or address. I know of a couple with children whose marriage broke up because the husband was emotionally unable to stay around while his wife underwent surgery. When she recovered she decided (rightly) that this man wasn't for her. On the other side of the ledger is another couple whose relationship became deeper because of the husband's devotion after his wife's quite sudden mastectomy. Trustworthiness and reliability can be both in deed and in the honesty with which one expresses one's feelings and intentions.

One cannot discuss such attitudes as commitment, trustworthiness, reliability, and honesty without asking about independence. This area may be more mishandled than any of these others. There is no ideal balance between dependence and independence because of the differences between couples—their life styles, ages, changing circumstances, etc. However, anyone who is committed to a relationship or is in the process of forming one ought to have a clear grasp of how much independence and dependence he requires and how much he is prepared to offer to the other.

This is an area of life style that is rapidly changing. Not so long ago, when divorces were hard to get, the standard of living was lower for the masses and many jobs for women were menial or nonexistent, people were thrown together under a suffocating blanket of emotional dependency. Generally speaking, in addition to sleeping together, they did everything else together. If one partner was independent, it would be a deliberate rebellion or provocation against the other. Today, life for many people is different.

It is not possible to be independent or to permit one's partner to be independent if one lacks inner resources. Another way of saying this is, if without someone to lean on and to occupy your feelings and activities you are lost, deprived, or empty, then you have no choice but to clutch. Conversely, a partner who has nothing without you is not going to let you out of sight emotionally or physically. An extreme but common example of this is the person who believes that "the world would end if I didn't marry." I have repeatedly stressed here, and in my psychotherapy practice, the importance of developing a part of one's life which (even if momentarily) is fulfilling and can be experienced without one's partner. Although it is not confined to housewives, this problem seems more frequent with them than with men. However, unmarried people also can be driven into a frenzy if there is no steady date or if they must spend an evening alone. I myself have found flower photography to be a hobby that lifts my spirits. I can go picture-taking alone or in company. Similarly for selecting slides for printing. While there can be only one eye behind the viewfinder, the resultant beauty can be shared with many. Thus, a hobby can develop both self-reliance and something worthwhile to share with others. Let me repeat, the person with no pleasures in life apart from his partner is likely to make the other person's commitment change to the feeling of being trapped.

It is emotional common sense to let the other person do his thing and to insist on your right to do your own thing. Do not erase yourself because of the other person's demands; you had also better decide whether you have been clutching so hard that you are defining your partner's identity as one of fulfilling your own dependency needs. The answer to one man's question can be a guide: "What is the difference between marriage and being a husband?" It seems to me that the difference is that when one is a husband (wife), one's individuality and special needs are recognized.

How does one recognize and defend against exploitation? The answer lies in the direction of feeling strong and able to withstand the consequences of a confrontation with the other person. A particularly unpalatable example might be the following: A woman reported that her father kept abusing her retarded son. His philosophy was "I'm basically a good guy and therefore you have to put up with what I do." She believed that if he was confronted her father would sulk and die. This exaggeration of either the strength or the vulnerability of offending adults can permit abuse, exploitation, degradation, and other sins against humanity. The basic problem is the person's feeling of dependency upon the offender. Therefore, one must steel oneself to the thought that it is honorable to fight against, to refuse to comply with, and to punish one who insists on degrading behavior. If necessary, hand them their marching orders. Post them to your emotional Siberia.

If you are selecting a mate, pick one who will let you be yourself and whom you respect enough to let him/her do his own thing. Find somebody with whom you share experiences and who likes to do the things you like to do.

Let us assume that you decide that you can live with your mate but you are genuinely frustrated or irritated. It is useful to separate the real from the unreal expectations. Perhaps you have been playing a sexual game and projecting or transferring qualities that do not really exist. Or you yourself have been reenacting one of those "inspiring" childhood stories which teach children about life through lofty tales of our royal ancestors.

It is also important to compromise and to be accepting. It is a truism that the failure of a relationship generally cannot be attributed to only one person. There are exceptions in the case of misrepresentation or criminal behavior. However, often enough the "victim" has been an accomplice for many years. I was told, when I was a psychologist at a state hospital in rural New York, that incest was frequent in some parts of that area. The mother might know about it for years but would not make a complaint against the old man until she had a personal grudge.

The question of assertiveness and security is a key one to observe. If you pick an inadequate partner to boost your ego, then you have nobody to blame for a whole parcel of complaints. Sensitivity in this area can be expressed in a variety of ways: "I wouldn't want a man who presents himself as insecure"; "I wouldn't want to be that strong and be on a pedestal." So who should build whose ego? This is a mutual responsibility, and frustration and rage are bound to ensue when one person cannot reassure the other in a moment of stress. It is equally frustrating to present the image of being always strong or always dependent. Circumstances will inevitably require that you change roles. If you cannot give or accept strength, reassurance, or affection, then your relationship has a built-in booby trap.

It is hard to experience meaningful sexual relationships when you have difficulty in expressing or accepting affection. It is frustrating as well to try to relate to a person who has such difficulties. Some people experience the exchange of affection to be an unwelcome commitment, or they feel unworthy or insincere. Perhaps the need is too great to fulfill, as in the case of the man whose father died when he was three, who was placed in an orphanage and searched continuously for fulfillment of his father's love. Another man was never fondled as a child. He kept looking for an older brother substitute, but couldn't find one because he had been told that other families were untrustworthy.

It is ruinous to a relationship not to express your feelings plainly and amply. Some people "make love and sex a guessing game without giving any clues." "To reject the verbal aspect of love is like turning out the lights." "A squeeze of the hand and a smile weren't enough to tell me that she liked the movie." These expressions of frustration may be contrasted with something like this: "You didn't call me for two weeks, but now that you're here it's great." If you have a good feeling, even if it's for that battleax you've been married to for fifty years, say it, tell it to her.

What can you do to enhance communications in order to hear the message of love or to make it possible? First, listen. Don't block out emotionally meaningful messages, even if they hurt. Then, respond to the point, if only with your own affection or hurt. Let the other person finish what he is saying. Interruptions are only a new source of conflict. Acknowledge mistakes; come on now, you're always making them. Ask questions. Don't be a mind reader. Encourage your partner to express his or her feelings. Finally, *do* something. The expression of concern may not be enough. When somebody hurts, remedy the situation.

If it is not emotionally possible to live with somebody, then you should consider separating. You will not be able to relate to somebody new until you are rid of the person who is hurting you. You might review the questionnaire in Chapter 7 to determine whether a relationship is meaningful or destructive or maybe a nothing.

Now, how to be a Good Lover!

17   *What Is a Good Lover?*

There are some people who would have the courage to answer this everlasting question, but I lack the requisite degree of presumption. My wariness is based on my belief that people's needs differ considerably and on the evidence of my eyes. People pair off in ways that surprise even the psychologist. Marriages survive that amaze friends who know the couple intimately. What I do is to ask large numbers of individuals what attracts them to others, what aids and what hinders their ability to express love, and what they actually consider a good lover. Finally, I will remind you to read "Mistakes Making Mates Miserable" so you know what to avoid.

I believe in listening to what people say, although I am aware of unconscious elements influencing vital actions. After all, it is the conscious verbal signals and images that are more easily reported and to which people attribute their choices. Further, these are the areas in which you can negotiate with your (intended) partner and express your feelings. It is a risky matter to try to establish a relationship and play psychoanalyst simultaneously!

It is useful to consider some of the following list of characteristics expressed by a group of adults. It will alert you to your own strengths and deficiencies and perhaps make you aware of some qualities important in good love relationships which you have

162

underestimated. Try to measure yourself and a lover against this expression of group feeling concerning what makes another person attractive:

"Physical appearance; voice; personality; warmth; mutual understanding; sexual gratification; enrichment; acceptance; lack of exploitation; ability to listen makes one relaxed; ability to make one feel very much alive; lack of nagging; tenderness and expression of love; romance and sex; genuinely interested and non-competitive; compatible and communicative; has qualities I want in myself; cheers me up; intellectuality; strengths; gives and receives warmth from the pleasure that I can give; confidence in self; realizes own positive traits; would feel it was worthwhile to have known me."

My personal reaction to this list is twofold: While it is pleasantly free of materialistic and unreal expectations, it also ignores considerations of life style which enhance satisfaction or could provide important irritations.

Again, how did a group of people respond to the question "What enhances your capacity to express love?" Since inability to express love is a common problem, you might consider some of these ways of helping your mate to be more expressive and thus create the circumstances in which your own capacity to express love is increased.

"When the person is unusually perceptive; when he does not see me as a stereotype; when I feel better about myself; when I can be of use; when I can fulfill a need of his; when the other person has a lot of feeling for me; when the other person doesn't disapprove of an open display of feelings; when I am relaxed; when there is a sense of trust; when he needs me and I need him; when he wants me and I want him; when there is a feeling of being accepted and comforted; when he treats me with gentleness and proper respect as a human being; when he knows me and doesn't expect something else; when he wants to do something for the other person; when the person understands my priorities."

A similar review of your relationship might follow this expression concerning the question "What hinders your ability to express love?" Remember, even nature needs a little help:

"Difficulty in asking for anything—I couldn't even ask for a hot dog because I'd feel like a pig; wanting the other person to make the first move; premature commitment is an encroachment on me; receiving more than giving; a crazy need for control and to push me around; fear of being rejected; asking for more than I am willing to give; not feeling I deserve affection from this person; fear of responsibility."

These various expressions and hindrances to loving behavior have already been discussed, and you might review some ways of increasing your positive qualities of expressiveness.

Before we approach directly the question "What is a good lover?", I would like to make a comment about women's experience of orgasm. Until quite recently, most professional persons in the area of human relationships would have stated that a woman's inability to have orgasm is *prima facie* evidence of serious sexual maladjustment. Orgasm for both sexes is a complex psychological-endocrinological-neural-muscular-vascular response. I suspect that it is more complex in the human female than the male and perhaps relatively minor circumstances can prevent a woman from achieving orgasm. It is useful to distinguish between the experience of orgasm (or its absence) and the reaction of either partner to that experience. In the days when it was assumed by some individuals that women were not interested in sexual experience, lack of orgasm was not noteworthy. Today, some concern is warranted, but caution must be exercised not to magnify the problem.

I repeat: it is difficult to achieve a proper perspective in one's sexual life. There are cases where a couple are happy in many respects but one or both partners are sexually dissatisfied. What sometimes occurs is that one partner assumes either that the other is sexually incompetent or disturbed or that he himself (or herself) is the culprit. Blame is experienced or attributed, and the degree of tension in the relationship increases substantially. In these changed circumstances, the degree of satisfaction and the capacity to please one's partner become hampered. The importance of lack of orgasm is exaggerated, and tension and dissatisfaction affect the emotional tone of the rest of the relationship.

What are the facts? Many women do not have orgasm with regularity. Of these, a large proportion state that they are sexually satisfied. It seems likely that their experience could be improved. However, it is the height of presumption to insist that they are not satisfied. If a couple experience sexual gratification when the woman is not achieving a climax, then one must be certain that the cure is not worse than the condition.

What, then, does emotional common sense suggest? Awareness of this problem might serve as an occasion to review the relationship. I suspect that this is rarely done except in a crisis, with arguments and recriminations. I believe that the couple should express their feelings about the condition and whether either of them feels that it is seriously hampering their sexual enjoyment. If this should be the case, then it would be useful to get both a medical and a psychotherapeutic consultation. Often a gynecologist or other physician cannot serve as a consultant in the psychological aspects of the sexual experience. However, there are sometimes remediable conditions which prevent a woman from achieving orgasm, and these should be ruled out. It might be useful for the medical consultant to provide education either for the man or for both partners. I know of one case where after years of marriage a husband could not locate his wife's clitoris. He was very rejecting of her sexuality because she refused variety. She, in turn, had refused to consult a gynecologist for years to see whether there was any medical condition interfering with her responsiveness. Both partners had attitudes which prevented them from enjoying sex, and the bedroom became a battlefield.

Being a good lover requires enthusiasm; it implies pleasing the partner. But it also requires a receptive attitude. It means that you expect and are willing to experience pleasure. Consider the complaint of one man that "a two-hour orgasm is a chore." There are lots of things that people can do if the orgasm comes more expeditiously. They can play Mozart duets on the piano, they can read poetry to each other, perhaps they can even go so far as to talk to each other. But holding back one's climax too long in order to control and gain the utmost from one's partner leads to self-destruction.

What, then, is a good lover? I think that a good lover is first of all knowledgeable and open-minded. Two books that I have found helpful are: *Human Sexual Response,* by William H. Masters and Virginia S. Johnson, and *The Encyclopedia of Sexual Behavior,* edited by Albert Ellis and Albert Abarbanel. Some reasonable balance is required between technique and the spiritual qualities of the relationship. There are plenty of sexual manuals available which can give you guides to variety and other ways of enhancing sexuality.

I think that a positive attitude toward sex and one's partner during the experience is also essential. To bring into the bedroom one's needs to be dependent, to express hostility, to dominate, to reject, and so forth, is an invitation to frustration. These unresolved problems lead to such disorders as premature ejaculation or potency problems in the man and frigidity or refusal to have sex in the woman. Leave your problems outside the bedroom or you will have to resort to the advice offered by one person: "Mark it on the calendar." Many couples start fights outside of bed, and in bed, but don't realize that they can resolve some fights in bed. If they could attempt to enjoy sex detached from their other conflicts, the bond between them would be strengthened. I have had patients who refused to take the sexual initiative or whose mates refused sex for long periods. In these cases, with the total breakdown of positive sexual feelings, the task of improving their relationship seemed hopeless.

What about the question of *commitment?* This can't be answered without reference to the decision to engage in exclusive or multiple relationships. If one or both partners are committed to the one-night stand, then being a good lover simply means having good technique, being sensitive to the wishes and feelings of the other, having the capacity to respond within the limits required by the other person, and similar technical considerations. But if one person will not have sexuality without knowing that there is a firm relationship, then frustration and retreat are likely to occur. For some, the opposite frame of mind holds: they do not wish to have a sense of obligation. Honest people will express their attitudes before they get undressed.

Then there's *consideration*. There are so many external circumstances which affect a person's sexuality. It is true that a larger proportion of men seem more sexually eager than women, but this is up to the point of encounter. Then the roles may become reversed or equalized. However, when a couple live together and do not have to engage in courtship rituals, they must have consideration for each other to a greater extent. An unmarried sexual pair can walk away from each other. Those who live together (with or without benefit of clergy) bear the consequences of their sexual acts and those circumstances which lead up to them. The man who insists on sex prematurely without arousing his partner is likely to leave her frustrated and angry with him. The woman who stays up till one o'clock to watch television, because the TV set and the only air conditioner are in the bedroom, succeeds in depriving her husband both of sleep and sex and does not make a friend.

The sense of uniqueness is required by many. It is a curiosity of human nature that the most intimate of experiences can also be thoroughly impersonal. I am not speaking about calling out the name of your second husband at a critical moment with your third. Nor that familiar slap on the fanny used to tease a previous lover despite the outrage of Ms. Current Lover. I mean the moment-by-moment awareness of the feelings of one's partner, with whatever change of pace or personal expression are required to augment the experience and make the other person aware that you know he/she exists. One is reminded of the lady who was in a bomb shelter during the V-bomb attack on London. She was complaining to her neighbor that she didn't like sex. When the latter remonstrated that she had four young children, she said, "Yes, I close my eyes and think of England."

I think that expressiveness is also part of being a good lover. Let your partner know what you feel, what you enjoy, even what you don't like or want changed. Since your enjoyment is vital to both of you, assuming that the relationship is really viable, you cannot ignore any possibility of letting your partner know how he can please you, provided you are willing to be pleased! If you are pleased, say so, encourage more sex, let the good spirits affect all parts of your relationship.

Finally, *part of being a good lover is not being obnoxious.* Reread the list of avoidable mistakes which would turn off the most loving, eager partner. If you can change by yourself, do so immediately. If you recognize your self-destructive attitudes in this list, you may need to get some psychotherapeutic consultation, because these characteristics will affect first your life in bed and then your life out of bed.

In addition to self-destructive sexual games, there are harmful patterns which make living with a particular person a miserable experience. Check yourself out to see if you make any of these mistakes.

18 *Emotional Problems of Employment*

The area of employment is one of the most underestimated causes of stress and emotional disorders. The reasons are complicated and I will not be able to discuss them all. However, my purpose in this chapter is a very simple one: I want you to evaluate your job and to take whatever steps may be necessary to improve your adjustment to it. If necessary, *fire your supervisor* (I mean, quit!).

There may be some Marxist readers who will immediately cry that the employment problems of work are all due to the system. To them I say baloney! Keep on reading. It is perfectly true that there are vast inequities in our system. Not too long ago I was personally on an unemployment line and disqualified because I earned a measly few bucks in my private practice. No matter that my employer was a thief who stole from his clients, his workers, and the government. Well, to heck with complaining about the system. I didn't stay around while he didn't pay my fees. I quit. I did what I could do. In fact, I won a judgment against him in court and found it impossible to collect, though my lawyers made out quite nicely. But that is another story. I tell you this to show that I haven't been living in an ivory tower.

A job can be considered from the point of view of *working conditions and requirements, characteristics of the worker,* and *personal factors.* By working conditions and requirements I mean the duties, the salary, the degree of responsibility, the quality of supervision, the social relationships characteristic of the job and organization, the opportunities for advancement, and so on. The characteristics of the worker are his intelligence, his skills, his education, his preference for the kinds of people he wants to deal with and the role he wants to play, his attitude toward responsibility, his values, and so forth. Personal factors include travel time to the job, economic demands made on him, obligations which may make his salary inadequate, and other concurrent activities such as schooling, which enhance or detract from his performance.

Thus, adjustment to a job involves not only the skills and personality characteristics of the worker but how he relates to the peculiarities of a particular position and what non-employment factors influence his life. The transportation available to him and his family may play as important a role in his success as his own skills or the qualities of his supervisor. To select a career, or even a position, or to evaluate why you are uptight every day at the plant requires often as comprehensive a personal diagnosis as why you can't get along with your spouse or lover. Most people just grouse about it and do not make any changes which would improve their peace of mind.

As I review some of the key areas of vocational adjustment, you will notice that they overlap considerably with other seemingly more personal problems. However, there is one difference which has been repeatedly reported to me. Many people complain that the area of business is more dishonest than other areas of life. I personally found that there was more lying and cheating in a brief sojourn that I had made into a particular area of the business world than in over a decade of work in various institutions and colleges. What are some examples?

I know a salesman who dislikes the need always to be cheerful with his accounts. As he puts it, "I can't be myself." Other people feel that they cannot get honest appraisals of their work because of insecure supervisors. Another instance is the requirement to put in one's best efforts, even though there is a lack of identification with the company's product or services or the values which are represented.

A closely related area is that of supervision. A large proportion of supervisors, owners, and managers are either technically or emotionally incompetent. These people are in my opinion the great source of emotional discomfort arising from the job. They are also the cause of high prices, company failures, product dangers and inadequacies. Supervisory and management failure is one of the most costly social problems in this country. It is so because the reasons for a person's promotion, or seeking promotion, is frequently not love for excellence and capacity to perform supervisory duties. These people are frequently technically ineffective and unable to gain the cooperation of subordinates and colleagues. Supervisors are often promoted, transferred, or fired because of favoritism, company politics, and acquisition of unrelated divisions as a part of conglomerates formed by money managers. Incompetents are protected because to discharge them would be to admit error, or to acknowledge criminally selfish union policies, or to say that their work is really done by others.

The most familiar complaint is the arrogant attitude of supervisors. I remember that when I was a young psychologist working in state hospitals, the directors were known for their ruthlessness. People in recent memory had been fired for walking on the grass, instructed to live on hospital grounds when they owned homes in a nearby town, and comfortable quarters in the hospital had been changed to offices. These so-called psychiatrists had come up through the system and, instead of learning compassion in dealing with their fellow employees, had waited until they reached the top to compensate by heaping vengeance on those who were fellow sufferers. There are so many supervisors who scream, derogate, keep creative people from flourishing, devise or implement petty, tyrannical regulations, or are indifferent to the working conditions, wages, and spirits of those whose economic welfare has been entrusted to them. Many of these individuals at high levels look the other way when their subordinates mistreat those under them.

A somewhat different problem is presented by supervisors who are afraid to take any risks. They reject good suggestions or requests for compassionate personnel action because of fear. These great men are afraid to have their own supervisors turn them down. What is frequently inconsequential to them is reacted to as though it were a serious personal threat to themselves. Perhaps the fear of assuming authority causes them to look elsewhere when the genuinely disruptive employee interferes with the capacity of others to work, is unproductive, noisy, bullying, etc. Their insecurity causes them to sabotage the creative efforts of competent personnel, to keep outdated or destructive procedures, to hire, retain, and promote incompetents. Such supervisors typically do not keep their technical skills up to date through study or further schooling, nor do they encourage ambitious subordinates to work at the level of their capacity or upgrade the procedures of the department. If they are personally ambitious, though incompetent, they frequently steal the concepts of those working for them.

However, not all of the emotional discomforts of employment are due to supervisors. You, too, can behave in self-destructive ways. Among the most difficult areas of adjustment is the basic attitude. You recall that this is the tendency to act assertively, compliantly, or perhaps rebelliously. Do not misunderstand my remarks about supervisors to mean that I am opposed to authority. I am not opposed to authority as such. A healthy technological society depends on some individuals assuming a great deal of responsibility and authority. It depends on all individuals in one way or another bowing to the legitimate restrictions, instructions, and even orders of those who have been given or have assumed key roles. However, there are severe imbalances caused by the misuse of authority (arrogant or denied) by some and the excessive compliance, rebelliousness, or negligence of others. All of these attitudes are neurotic and destructive to the well-being of an organization, co-workers in that organization, and of the group's capacity to provide goods and services for the community.

The reader ought to consider his own attitude as well as to try to understand the effect of the attitude of his supervisors, colleagues, and subordinates on him. If you find yourself always assuming an authoritarian, know-it-all approach to the people you deal with at the plant or office, then it is likely that you are either arrogant or rebellious. You are probably transferring the superior attitude inculcated in you as a child or developed by you in defense against feelings of worthlessness. On the other hand, if you are uncomfortable in exercising authority—e.g., giving orders, correcting mistakes, maintaining discipline, firing goof-offs—then you feel unworthy of assuming responsibility. You must either develop self-confidence or move to a position that does not feed these feelings of inadequacy. But don't stay there and suffer or cause others to suffer.

Another emotional problem that causes a great deal of discomfort is insecurity. It is possible to be talented and productive and yet *feel* that one is performing inadequately. The idea of personal worth and vocational success are frequently mixed up. The child who is raised to feel valueless carries this self-image to school and job. Conversely, a failure at school or work may mean to the person that he is really no good. Since low self-esteem reduces likelihood of success, a cycle arises of discouragement, hopelessness, and then genuine lack of progress or outright failure.

Today, with inflation, unemployment, and high interest rates, both private and public employers place a great emphasis on productivity. Thus, on-the-job training is likely to be scarce. Highly qualified individuals have been fired due to the business recession and have to compete with less skilled people. The latter may be bumped downward to even less remunerative, interesting, or skilled jobs. The talented may be underemployed and the untalented out of work or doing unexpectedly menial tasks.

Another cause of economic inefficiency and damaged morale is discrimination. Our country is notorious for this. In turn the Italians, Irish, Jews, blacks, and Puerto Ricans have suffered from it. I know one non-Jew who was discriminated against because he *looked* like a Jew.

What about discrimination against women? There is no doubt that a talented woman finds it harder than a man to get into technical schools and to obtain responsible positions and advancement in many industries and particular companies. There is enough reality to the complaints about women employees to cause difficulty for the talented, ambitious female. I personally have had very unpleasant experiences with female supervisors (male also) and would prefer not to work for a woman. Many men and women feel the same way. In part, however, the prejudice against promoting women is the small child's resentment against his mother and teachers. However, I believe that the excessive struggle for women's success as well as the social pressures which cause them to seek lower goals as children create personality problems which add to the normal difficulties of being a competent supervisor. The only answer is to insist that all promotions be based on talent. The implication is that some women, some members of minority groups really might not have the personality to be promoted. But it is self-destructive to prevent those who are technically and emotionally competent people from getting ahead. Thus, at some time in the future, every individual would be encouraged to develop his talents and could plan on increasing his responsibilities without fear or frustration due to prejudice.

What about the meaningfulness of one's work? It is commonplace that the need for craftsmanship, for individual skills, has been so reduced as to create a serious mental-hygiene problem. Workers on automated motorcar assembly lines go berserk or deliberately sabotage vehicles in order to obtain excitement. There are enormous numbers of repetitive service positions like sorting letters, selling stamps or subway tokens, punching computer data cards, filing correspondence, etc. Many of the people filling these jobs have the intelligence and emotional stamina to handle more complex, demanding positions. Even in large organizations whose functions have high social value, the proportion of tedious, routinized jobs is very large. Some people respond to boredom with depression. Busy work is sometimes created to justify the empire-building of dishonest managers.

Most people want some degree of recognition. They want to be praised, to receive economic and emotional rewards for their services. However, this is sometimes a frustrating trap. Recognition may be sought not as a personal reward but as a vindication. Recognition means that parents were wrong in telling you that you would never be a success, that your wife is wrong in thinking you a failure, or that your children will consider you a hero. A normal degree of wish for success and esteem can also be frustrated by the routine nature of one's position or the negativistic attitudes of jealous supervisors.

What, then, is the emotional common sense approach to employment?

1. *Do not expect justice.* There are many factors which go into success. Hard work and talent are only two of them. You should be prepared to experience favoritism, arrogance, cowardice, lying, broken promises, illegal activities, being stabbed in the back, bad luck, poor timing, difficult economic conditions, and any other mishap that occurs to people.

2. *Be prepared to work hard.* Earn an honest day's pay. If you have genuine reason to be dissatisfied, emotional common sense requires that you not be a patsy forever, and you must be prepared to change jobs or get a transfer. Therefore, you must be able to convince your new employer, either with or without a reference, that you are a capable worker and interested in producing regardless of personal discomfort. Work, but look around.

3. *Know your own talents and capacities.* While there may be economic emergencies which force you to take any particular position available, you are not required to serve there for life! There are characteristics you have that will be natural for some jobs and render you uncomfortable or cause you to bomb out on others. At the end of this chapter is a Self-Appraisal form for

Career Advancement. It will help you, but it might be still necessary for you to get some professional guidance from a vocational or industrial psychologist.

4. *Be yourself.* Whether you are a salesman, a clerk, a manager or a professional person, you have a style of living which can be expressed on a job and which makes you comfortable and doesn't antagonize others. If you believe that you are required to be excessively compliant, be more forthright. If the supervisors or clientele with whom you deal require a hypocritical, plastic manner and this is not you, then consider whether you are in the wrong occupation or with the wrong firm. Lamb and Turner, in *Management Behavior,* describe an executive in part as follows: "A limitation in relation to the business world is that he is straightforward, unsophisticated and sincere to an exceptional degree. This, in combination with his lack of purposeful drive toward clear objectives, makes him unsuited for situations requiring political maneuverings and subtle tactics."

5. *Don't let yourself be bullied or abused.* Always remember that many of your supervisors have been appointed to their position or have wheedled their way there not because they are competent but rather because they are acting out infantile feelings of inferiority. Therefore, should you find yourself in a position in which you are being pushed around needlessly, then fight back. You will rarely be fired, and if so it will be worth it. Many individuals suffer from neurotic feelings of guilt. If they are supervisors, they become arrogant in the hope of arousing anger and subsequent punishment for their feelings of guilt. They hope to feel better when limits are placed on their hostility. If they are subordinates, then they permit *it* to happen for the same reason: It is coming to them anyway. Do not get into a neurotic guilt-provocation-punishment cycle. You must preserve your self-respect and not have the remainder of your day and free time ruined because of rumination over being abused. If you know your organization you may be able to call the situation to somebody's attention discreetly and in a constructive way. If you try and fail, then you

must either fight or run. Remember the Chinese proverb already mentioned: "Of the thirty-six ways of averting disaster, running away is the best." Do not let your head hang in the noose.

6. *Show initiative.* It is not terrible to have a suggestion refused or a request not granted. Fear of this is a mark of the insecure bureaucrat. Try to put your imprint on your department. If you cannot do so, then you ought to take stock. Perhaps your ideas are less effective than you believe. In this case, you require more experience or education. However, if this is not the case, prepare yourself for a new organization which can use some fresh blood.

7. *Keep your education up to date.* If you are resigned to tedious, repetitive jobs, getting your jollies completely in your free time, then skip to the next section. However, I presume that most readers of this book are in positions requiring some skills. Believe me, there is nothing that gets out of date faster than knowledge. This obviously means that you must participate in in-service training conscientiously. If this is not available, then you must make the sacrifice to study at home or at an institution. If you cannot bear to tear yourself away from golf, tennis, the kiddies or that number you've been courting, then the price you pay will be very precisely determined. Your career will slow down, and people no more competent than you will get ahead and earn more money and have fewer frustrations in the professional area.

8. *Be an effective leader.* I learned an invaluable idea in ROTC. A leader performs two functions simultaneously: he performs the mission, and he looks out for the welfare of his men. If you believe that you can drive the slaves under you or look out for your own interests without reference to your subordinates' welfare, you may possibly succeed. But your future is also limited. You will go nowhere because your staff will perform in ways that do you no credit. You are probably stuck in your current job forever. Further, you will live forty hours a week in an environment in which you are despised. I have had supervisors who drove the staff while spending their own time reading cheap novels (feet up on radiator) or contacting their stockbrokers. Had their own supervisors

taken the interest in the effectiveness of the department, then these people would have been fired or forced to be productive. Instead, I chose to leave because my own well-being forbade me to be exploited by these selfish incompetents.

9. *Be courageous.* As I pointed out before, it is generally wise to fight back if you are bullied. What some people use as a guide are statements like this to their supervisors: "Fire me, but don't abuse me. . . . Fire me or trust me." I had the chief of a clinic who was on an on-time kick call me in and ask me where I was at eight o'clock that morning. I looked him in the eye and asked him where he had been at four-thirty yesterday. He went screaming to my immediate chief and complained about my attitude, but he never asked me again what time I arrived. *He knew I was watching him.* Confront the bully. As one person put it, "What's more important, the dollars or how you feel?" If your problem is anxiety rather than a person, the best way to eliminate the anxiety is to force yourself to do what you have to do anyway. Should your problem be a feeling of inadequacy, then regard competition as a healthy, constructive, and indeed necessary way to increase productivity and exercise your mental muscles. If you feel discriminated against, then the first thing to do is to determine whether your efforts and the quality of your work really warrant a promotion or raise. Then ask for it. Finally, if necessary, go to the appropriate governmental agency and demand that the laws be enforced. After all, there may be some young, energetic, hungry fellow there just aching to make a name for himself through helping a deserving person like you against that monstrous corporation.

10. *Blow your own horn.* If you want recognition, let people know what you have done. Better yet, make sure that your supervisors' supervisors know what you are doing. I have a patient who does creative design work for a famous industrial laboratory. He does not take the time to write up his own reports for his company's marketing efforts. Thus, when others do so, he becomes the anonymous (though capable) creator. If you have a supervisor who

gets nervous when he hears that you are capable and have initiative, size up the situation. If he has a vested interest in keeping you down or stealing the credit from you, move.

11. *Become involved.* Pick a trade or a position which is something that you can value. If your qualifications are temporarily routine, then go into a company, industry, or institution that is performing work that you can take pride in.

12. *Have a parachute.* There are some people who get very uptight when I advise that the best way to handle a job which makes you unhappy is to quit it. They feel that this is the irresponsible counsel of a well-heeled private practitioner. I have taken the risk of going into private practice because I saved sufficient money to tide me over in an emergency. I have an opportunity to hear how people spend their money, and very often they have more optional funds than they know about or care to admit. It is vital that you have a number of months' expenses available in cash so that you can meet emergencies, one of which is getting fired or laid off or deciding to quit. If you have a bigger house, an expensive wife, and more children than you can afford, you lack emotional common sense. Have a parachute. Cut down on your expenses. You do not have to remain in an unnecessarily frustrating position which ruins your peace of mind if you have the wherewithal to survive while you look around.

It will be helpful in evaluating your employment situation if you seriously consider the following "Self-Appraisal for Career Advancement" which I have devised for use in executive counseling.

SELF-APPRAISAL FOR CAREER ADVANCEMENT

Frustrations and difficulties in present (or recent) position: List all frustrations and difficulties. State those which have caused you to seek a change. Include anything which jeopardizes your present position, blocks suitable advancement, or otherwise causes you to be dissatisfied.

Career goals: (Be specific)
Immediate:

Long-Range:

List those personality characteristics which you believe affect the achievement of your career goals:
Strengths: Personality characteristics which enhance your efficiency and make you valuable to an employer. Include those for which you have been commended or complimented and those which add to your enjoyment of the job or positively affect the people with whom you have contact. Give a brief illustration of each, if you can:

1.

2.

3.

4.

5.

Weaknesses: These are personality characteristics which reduce your efficiency, create situations in which you function poorly or are uncomfortable. Include those for which you have been criticized or which seem to affect negatively the people with whom you have contact. Give a brief example or explanation of each:

1.

2.

3.

4.

5.

Characteristics of the position in which you could function effectively and with satisfaction to yourself:
Structure: A structured position is one in which there are company policies and regulations affecting the way a job is to be carried out, where the goals and methods are precisely known and the procedures are clearly defined. An unstructured position is one in which the worker devises his own procedures, and the methods may vary considerably from time to

time. How structured should a position be for you to function with the greatest efficiency and personal satisfaction?

Loosely structured   Moderately structured   Highly structured
Comments:

Supervision: What characteristics of a supervisor would tend to create conditions in which you can function most efficiently and with the greatest satisfaction? What characteristics of a manager are particularly troublesome to you? If applicable, describe the best supervisor you ever had.

Illustrate or give examples that will support your choices:

Indicate any sensitivities or limitations you have:

Indicate any area which your education is deficient in and which will hamper your career advancement:

Your Attitude Toward Being a Supervisor:
Do you have a preference for or against supervision of others? (Explain) What is the greatest number of individuals you have ever supervised:

Nature of the position where it occurred:

Model of Preferred Relationships on a Peer Level:
There are a number of different relationships with peers—i.e., individuals whom you do not supervise and who do not supervise you but to whom you may relate on a job. List first three preferences in order (1, 2, 3).

     Committee: Exchanging ideas and sharing responsibilities with several others.

     Loner: Staff work; also primary responsibility for carrying out a task without requiring substantial aid from others.

     Consultant/Trouble Shooter: Serving as an expert to help others carry out tasks assigned to them.

     Liaison/Coordination: Conveying information, instructions, problems, etc., from one department to another without having responsibility for actually carrying out the task.

     Teacher/Trainer: Educating others on how to carry out assigned tasks with greater skills without direct responsibility for performance.

     Sales: Internal and external contacts necessary to the development of satisfied customers (new and old).

     Public Relations: Internal and external contacts to promote corporate image.

Industrial Relations: Developing employee morale, interpreting company policy, etc.

Rate yourself in the areas listed below. Compare yourself to those businessmen, professionals, executives, teachers, etc., you have known and against whose performance yours could be reasonably compared. Remember that individuals vary in ability, so that in any group not everybody can be above average; some are definitely below average. Furthermore, the ratings of the different abilities of a particular person may vary considerably. To help you form an accurate self-evaluation, imagine that your rank in one hundred individuals is to be determined. Then decide where you rank for each of the abilities listed below:

Rank in 100	Highest 5%	Above Average 76%–95%	Average 25%–75%	Below Average 6%–24%	Lowest 5%
Conceptualizing	———	———	———	———	———
Planning	———	———	———	———	———
Organizing	———	———	———	———	———
Administering	———	———	———	———	———
Delegating	———	———	———	———	———
Negotiating	———	———	———	———	———
Supervising	———	———	———	———	———
Leading	———	———	———	———	———
Training	———	———	———	———	———

19 *Decision-Making, Productivity, and Creativity*

For anyone who does not live on a day-to-day basis, the difference between peace of mind or even prosperity, and the sense of being harried and ineffectual is effective decision-making. I include productivity under this heading because in the real world happiness is achieved by those who do and create and not by those who lead the life of consumers. Emotional common sense means making correct, realistic decisions based on your needs. Self-destructiveness is wasting your efforts through lack of discipline or working for others exclusively.

Here is a plan for augmenting productivity through effective decision-making. I believe that it is applicable to a variety of important life situations, whether preparing a term paper for school (or even a doctoral dissertation), deciding on a career, developing an important project for your employer, buying a house, or whatever. It is a strategy for increasing your effectiveness, and the areas in which you apply it will be determined by your ingenuity and devotion to emotional common sense.

Let me state that it works! By using these techniques I have been able to write this book in less than three months, earn a living, and have some fun. However, be warned that to tackle a project of this size also required considerable years of preparation

183

and thought. But when I felt like it, I had a way to do it. Also, there were important professional reasons for me to write at this time, and I knew that I had to make some sacrifices of time to forward my career. Now, to work!

1. *Know yourself.* No effective decision can be made without knowing your own personality and capacity. Furthermore, you ought to know intimately what are your frustrated *needs*. It is self-destructive to commit yourself to a large project involving time, and perhaps the expenditure of money, unless it definitely fulfills your needs. If recognition is vital to you, then don't get buried in a bureaucracy. If you require love, then don't become tied to a doctoral adviser or employer who enjoys being critical. It is also essential that you work according to your *values*. If a close relationship to your family is most important to you, then a position requiring travel or extensive overtime will provide stress. If you are an honest person, then an assignment requiring you to invent results will be intolerable, as was discovered by an aircraft manufacturer's technician instructed to write fraudulent results for the tests of the brake system of a military aircraft. You must also *know your limits.* Do you wish to be projected up to your "level of incompetence"? As set forth by Peter and Hull in *The Peter Principle,* each level of work requires different characteristics. After a certain degree of success, one may be assigned tasks that are beyond one's competence and even then not be fired. The officeholder spends his life in a variety of self-deceiving, self-justifying tasks to hide his inability to do the job. What is your *capacity to work?* If you know that you lack self-discipline, then you must either overcome it or avoid the stress and frustration of assuming responsibilities you can't fulfill. Since most tasks require working with others, you should decide whether you are a loner, preferring to work in isolation, or what the social circumstances are in which you do your best efforts. The self-appraisal questionnaire that I devised in doing career counseling with hundreds of executives and professionals will help you to select the situation in which you are likely to be most effective. There are very different kinds of relationships between people in various kinds of positions (see

"Model of Preferred Relationships," p. 181). You should also take into account your preferred *basic attitude*, whether assertive, compliant, indecisive, or perhaps resistant to authority.

2. *Know your organization.* Practically all decisions require you to function within or through an organization. If you have built a better mousetrap, people won't beat a path to your door in the forest unless you set up a fine marketing organization yourself or hire one. If you are functioning within an organization, get to know its written and unwritten regulations and customs. Find out about the communications, power centers, and sensitivities of its members. If you function through an organization, for example, put your house up for hire or call in a consultant such as a lawyer, accountant, advertising agency, make certain that these helpers can function well and *place your interests at least on a par with their own, if not first.*

3. *Gather information.* To make decisions for yourself or others on the basis of inadequate information is to court disaster. Are you going to college, selecting a marriage partner, setting up a company, picking a job, designing part of a machine? How will your production fit into the whole? What is needed? What are the written or unwritten requirements? Check the specifications, catalogue, personnel procedures, laws, or customs. If the task is complex, try to get all the necessary information before you devise your plan. However, there is probably a point of diminishing returns when it ceases to pay to gather more information because it will delay initiation of the venture, or not all of the data is sufficiently useful. Do not gather information as a delaying substitute for action based on fear. Nevertheless, to make decisions without gathering information may be catastrophic. Other qualities of leadership cannot compensate for this lack. Above all, take into consideration the facts from all parties concerned. How many times have I seen stupid policies implemented, or potentially adequate policies sabotaged, because directives came from On High downward, without asking the opinions of us slaves who had to carry out the orders.

4. *Develop objectivity.* Let me illustrate two cases where lack

of objectivity could have been disastrous. In one, a manager got himself fired because of embezzlement. He succeeded in getting a new, potentially responsible position but was in great fear of losing it and being unable to obtain a new one. He became extremely cautious in order not to make mistakes or give his employers any reason to explore his background. I pointed out to him that *instead of trying to do the task he was making decisions as a guilty man.* This proved very helpful to him in going about his duties in a relaxed, goal-oriented way. A lawyer violated the third principle, not gathering sufficient information, as he prepared a lease for a client in a commercial area with which he was not familiar. He stated: "I became petrified and stopped thinking productively. I accepted the fact that I may have damaged my client and started to solve the problem." Thus, *he no longer acted as a frightened man.*

As you proceed toward making and carrying out a decision, you must consider your *level of enthusiasm.* The first flush of determination may conceal the fact that a problem is insoluble, that the cooperation of others is required, and that you yourself may not have the intellectual, economic, and spiritual resources to complete the job. One man left the Army and decided to do some graduate work because he had the benefits of the GI Bill. He had exhausted his benefits when he was halfway through to his Ph. D. He started his doctorate because his father thought it would be a good idea. For the next half dozen years he was hung up because he didn't want to drop his credits, nor did he care to invest any more time in an area which was no longer of interest to him and had no appreciable material value to compensate for the time involved. Further, he had gathered far more information than he could use and to organize it properly would involve a great deal of additional unnecessary time (from the viewpoint of achieving his particular goal, the doctoral degree). His wife complained, the house was full of his papers, and his social life was contaminated by the thought that he ought to be home writing! More about him later.

5. *Set achievable goals.* There should be a consistent pattern including real needs, deeply felt values, and the means of satisfying them—i.e., achievable goals. Some people are dominated by the trauma of their childhood and set goals for themselves which are beyond their capacities, or damaging to others, or meet the needs of their parents rather than themselves. Others have been so disappointed by life that they chronically underachieve—that is, do not even set goals and obtain satisfactions which are within their capacity to obtain readily. *The riskiest goal of all is to be famous or glamorous.* After all, this is an insidious form of dependence on the opinions of others. If (secretly) you wish to be famous, then I suggest that the best path is through meritorious achievement. I also suggest that when you get to be famous you will have paid through the nose because of the sacrifice of family, friends, and fun. Let us take the advice again of Albert Einstein: "The only way to escape the personal corruption of praise is to go on working. One is tempted to stop and listen to it. The only thing is to turn away and go on working. Work. There is nothing else."

6. *Create an overall plan.* The best way to achieve with economy of time, effort, and money is to see the picture as a whole before you begin. It is true that circumstances change and some difficulties are unforeseen, so that the final achievement may differ significantly from its initial formulation. However, it is my experience that a definite framework should exist at all times in a project, and it can be modified as you proceed. With such an outline, you constantly keep in mind the various aspects of the work. As you become bogged down in one way, you can simultaneously work on another aspect of the problem and solve it.

How did I write this book? The original idea came a year before I started to write. Finally I decided that my advice to a patient about writing a few pages a day could just as well apply to myself. I selected and revised chapter headings. Then I organized around the chapter headings about eighty different sets of notes that I had taken at discussion groups and reassigned each set of notes as I exhausted material appropriate to a given chapter. As the material developed, I rearranged it and added new topics and combined others. For example, with this particular chapter, it took me about two hours to gather and review the appropriate materials. Then it took another hour and a half to devise an outline, the present one being the fourth attempt. Even as I type, I find myself changing some of the details because of connections that were not apparent before I began.

7. *Don't scatter your efforts.* There is no substantial, worthwhile project that you can achieve unless you control and limit your investment of time. This implies, first, *limiting the number of projects* that you work on simultaneously and, secondly, *making sacrifices* of transient pleasures and goals in order to complete the more valuable extensive project. Everybody has a certain limit beyond which he cannot work, or a number of activities beyond which he cannot concentrate his efforts. Therefore, you must decide what are the limits of your stamina, your facilities, and your intellect. Then limit your output in such a way as to respect these limitations.

8. *Select priorities.* Having decided the amount of output that you are capable of, you must determine which projects are important to you and which can be eliminated as inconsequential. Then, if you are to be an achiever, a producer, and not a frustrated dreamer, you must *commence activities in terms of their priorities and put off or eliminate activities which do not forward your plan.* This may mean going to school instead of bowling; it may mean painting instead of going to a movie; it may mean eliminating minor tasks to save yourself for the big one. You will accomplish nothing unless you can decide what is important to you and refuse to spend much time on that which is time-wasting or distracting. It is possible that at particular times your goals may override family, friends, and amusement. If you cannot make this particular sacrifice, then it is better that you give up the project and live your life as enjoyably as you can.

9. *Develop a self-confident attitude.* The most important difference between people who succeed and those who don't, capacities

and opportunities being equal, is their degree of self-confidence. The self-confident person strikes out boldly, takes risks, and overcomes obstacles. The person with low self-esteem thinks like a failure and does not begin to cope with obstacles. *No self-confidence, no risk, no overcoming frustration, no success.* Remember that everybody makes mistakes, and if you are qualified for your position, then you can survive errors unless your employer is irrational. If you are really unqualified, you have but two choices: change jobs or improve your skills. If you have a fear of failure, you can help to overcome it through following this guide to decision-making and productivity, particularly concept #5, "Set Achievable Goals." If you are afraid of competition, then concept #1, "Know Yourself," is the key. In this way, by developing your own skills and using them as a guide, you will be productive. Competition is frequently a whip held by exploitative teachers and supervisors, anyway.

10. *Create the proper atmosphere.* There is a particular ambiance which will enhance your productivity. Some people work best with music blaring. After I started my graduate studies my ability to concentrate was impeded by unnecessary sounds. An accountant just told me of resigning a job after five weeks where he had been hired to reorganize an office. Radios, eating, the flirting of the managers at the water cooler, all made it impossible for him to work. There are many inconsiderate and stupid people who do not care about the feelings of others or are indifferent to their capacity to work. If you are working in an institution, make your demands clear for satisfactory working conditions. Do not let others jeopardize your job and your capacity to create and produce. If you have something to do at home, such as study, write, or paint, get a working space for yourself. Do not let family or neighbors interfere. If they do, *create pain for them.* If your needs are legitimate and you pursue them without trampling others' rights and productivity, then be forthright in creating that atmosphere in which you can work. I wrote this book largely after 11:30 P.M. because of the fewer interruptions and the silence of the

streets. I was less than cordial with those who called me after that
hour. I traded my fatigue for the ability to work uninterruptedly.
Others report a variety of techniques for enhancing their productivity. One woman, born in Poland, had her name changed by her
parents. When she resumed the original name, she became more
productive. It has been reported that sharing responsibility is
helpful. Some require being prodded, in which case only certain
kinds of positions will permit them to do their best work. One man
stated that he needed a sense of kinship with others, so he did his
work in the public library.

11. *Divide the project into parts.* It is very easy to be overwhelmed by the amount of effort required in any worthwhile
project. After I completed my Ph.D. courses and dissertation, I felt
that *even I couldn't conceptualize the total amount of effort,* particularly when I took into consideration that I had required the
cooperation of numerous other people. In concept #4, "Develop
Objectivity," I related the story of a man who became bogged
down in a large doctoral dissertation. What enabled him to make
a breakthrough was my suggestion that he decide in advance how
much work he could put in on a given day without strain. He said,
"One hour." I advised him to work one hour in the morning and
one hour in the evening and to enjoy the rest of the day. This
advice was also helpful with a young woman suffering from the
same difficulty. By working *only that amount of time in which you
can be productive* will you be able to get going. Both of these
individuals subsequently increased their productivity to the point
where they not only worked more hours but finished their disser-
tations satisfactorily. Whether it is a set number of hours, or writing a certain number of pages, or practicing a difficult section of
a sonata, know your limits, respect them, and then stop. Enjoy
yourself the rest of the time, or do less demanding work.

12. *Exercise self-discipline.* This section was more or less cov-
ered under #8, "Select Priorities." However, it is worth repeating. Without self-discipline, you will get nowhere. Whether you
study, go to an office, or work at home, there will be many distrac-

tions. Some of them will be created by people who have already made it or have no ambitions of their own. If you wish to get ahead, you will have to work and not play. While there is a definite value to having cordial relationships with the people around you, both for their sake and for achieving your own goals, do not permit yourself to be distracted from expeditiously following your overall plan because *others want to play when you ought to work.*

13. *Have fun.* The same comment applies to this section. It is most important that whatever your stage of life, you develop some interests, hobbies, or friends, which will give you something to look forward to. Quite possibly, even under the most strenuous demands, there is some activity close to home that will relieve your spirits and clear your mind. Don't be a dull dog!

14. *Follow through.* Most projects require the cooperation of others. It makes no difference whether you are a manager, a military officer, a free-lance writer who works through an agent, you cannot do it alone. I recently sued somebody, won the case, only to discover that my braggart lawyer did not register the judgment, whatever that is. I immediately took the case away from him and gave it to another lawyer to collect my money. The first scoundrel was too busy to look after my interests properly. Set up some kind of a schedule for others to comply realistically with what they have agreed to do, or have been assigned, and then you should follow through. *Make sure that your requirements are being met.* If your helpers cannot, or will not, meet those requirements, find somebody who will. *Make no assumptions concerning the productivity of others.*

15. *Set reasonable standards.* There are two ways of looking at standards. The first is the overall scope of the project—i.e., how big or complicated it is. This has to be kept within limits, utilizing concepts #1, #2, and #5, "Know Yourself," "Know Your Organization," and "Set Achievable Goals." Once the overall plan is decided on, there are degrees of excellence with which it can be implemented. In most circumstances, it is more important that a project be done merely well rather than perfectly. To expect

perfection is to invest a degree of time and effort which may prevent completion. We will discuss timeliness below, but pay attention to quality here. Generally, only in highly engineered projects—e.g., aerospace and military weapons systems, or such various artistic/technical works as cutting gems—is perfection required. There are world-renowned musicians, respected and loved by public critics, whose work occasionally lacks technical perfection demonstrated by others, but the scope and feeling are overwhelming. Other artists became renowned because of their precision, but most of the really great ones have qualities of passion as well. In short, unless the task really requires it, perfectionism may be a self-destructive attitude. It is based, generally, on feelings of guilt, meeting the unreasonable standards of parental figures, or self-vindication for feelings of inadequacy.

16. *Obtain criticism.* It is necessary to obtain feedback concerning your progress. An open mind has various advantages. At the beginning is the most important time to gain the opinions of others. As you develop your project, others may be able to point out facets that you did not know about or pitfalls in your intended procedure. Subsequently, as you have committed your resources, it is less useful to gain basic insights unless you have actually blundered or fallen into unexpected severe difficulties. As you proceed, what others observe is an increasingly finished product. You can select individuals who will give you objective comments. This will relate to quality, meeting the needs of the organization or marketplace, timeliness, receptivity of those for whom it is intended, morale of subordinates, attitudes of co-workers, and so on. Sometimes, useful criticism can even be obtained from those who are basically negativistic or poorly intentioned. I don't like criticism at all, but I have disciplined myself to listen to it if I feel that there may be some truth in the message. I brace myself and try to learn about my performance. If, however, I consider the potential criticizer to be a liar or deviously interested in the well-being of some other party, I avoid him like the plague and don't bother to make any excuses for doing so.

17. *Be timely.* You can waste years of efforts, opportunities for promotion, and in many ways court disaster by not having your work done on time. We live in a complicated, integrated society. Generally, one person's performance depends on someone else's work. If your work is not ready, then the next link of the chain is delayed. Furthermore, you will be on the carpet. When I worked at the Veterans Administration, I used to have to help prepare a time-consuming monthly report. *There was no way I could get out of doing it.* Therefore, although I generally had other duties I would have preferred doing, I got my report in (generally) on time. By not holding up the work of the collector of these data I maintained myself on good terms with him, avoided anxiety, and kept out of predictable trouble.

I can suitably conclude this section on effective decision-making with a quotation from Harold Lamb's *Charlemagne:* "Do not wait for an age of perfect minds. It will never come."

A COMMENT ON CREATIVITY

There is no substitute for hard work if you wish to be creative. With hardly any exceptions, the greatest painters, writers, composers have worked day and night. They have buried themselves in their profession. As I was reading Darwin's *preliminary report* of his scientific findings *(The Voyage of the Beagle),* I was struck by his scholarship at the age of twenty-two. He did not publish *The Origin of Species* until twenty-eight years had passed (1859), including thirteen months and ten days of "hard labor" on the manuscript itself. Artur Rubinstein says that if he does not practice the piano for one day, he knows it; if he doesn't practice for two days, his agent knows it; and if he doesn't practice for three days, the public knows it. If you wish to be creative but are unable to work hard, *forget your impossible dream.* Don't frustrate yourself. Just enjoy life.

20 *If All Else Fails: Choosing a Psychotherapist*

Choosing a competent professional person is an extremely difficult task in any area, since the nature of the relationship and the degree of success are frequently a matter of confidentiality between consultant and client. This is particularly so in the area of psychotherapy. Therefore, I will try to make you aware of some of the issues in undertaking psychotherapy, if you decide that this is necessary to break your cycle of self-destructive behavior.

There are many types of psychotherapy and, as a consequence, many roads toward becoming a competent practitioner. You should also be aware that the definition of psychotherapeutic practice is vague both conceptually and legally, so that it is possible for incompetents, crooks, and charlatans to practice and to mistreat their clients. The issues are so great in New York State right now that there is a mud-slinging campaign, firing of individuals from the alternate camp, threats of legal suit, interdisciplinary quarrels, and so forth. Thus, the person who wishes to undergo psychotherapy has to be cautious in picking a suitable practitioner.

What is psychotherapy? Psychotherapy is a means of changing behavior by verbal influence, without the use of medicines or physical agents, so that the individual can adapt better by his own criteria or by those of the more powerful figures who sent him.

Most people enter psychotherapy because they feel worthless and they want to feel better. From here on, I will refer only to the situation of the self-referred adult who is unhappy, feels that he is contributing something to his own downfall, and voluntarily seeks psychotherapeutic assistance.

There are many varieties of psychotherapy. Some of them represent the products of the most talented minds of the twentieth century, and some are cultish products of grandiose messiah types. Thus, the first phase of determining which psychotherapist to use is his breadth of training and open point of view. Those who are narrow-minded or those who espouse the universal value of specific techniques may succeed in helping a few individuals for whom their procedures are suitable. The remainder run the risk of either being damaged emotionally or having appropriate psychotherapy delayed should they feel discouraged in treatment. *Remember, there is no psychological theory, including my own, that is applicable in understanding and treating all people.*

It is important to distinguish between the *patient's goals* and the *therapist's goals.* The patient's goals are to feel better, to be more productive and creative, to enjoy better relationships with family, friends, colleagues, to have a better sex life. The patient will probably be able to proceed more effectively in psychotherapy when he enters into some situation of stress and then tries to clarify what he wants from life, struggling to gain the insight and self-discipline necessary to communicate his feelings to the therapist. The therapist generally works to develop a therapeutic relationship in which the patient can achieve his own goals. Other therapist goals may be a warm atmosphere in which a relationship of confidence can develop, the correction of errors of behavior and the increased understanding that is called insight, and offering various educational procedures so that the patient can better understand his reactions to people and their feelings about him.

Psychotherapy can be divided into varieties of *individual* and *group therapy.* The earliest scientific form of psychotherapy was psychoanalysis, the creation of Sigmund Freud and his many talented disciples. There are also historically important alternatives that are still being practiced and whose adherents maintain important training institutes: Individual Psychology of Alfred Adler and Analytical Psychology of Carl Jung. What these theories have in common, which is denied by many newer practitioners (though not by myself), is the importance of historical events in warping the capacity of an individual to adapt and to see the world realistically. Many of the newer theorists insist that only the person's current feelings, distortions, and attitudes are relevant to the treatment problem. It seems to me that I would not like arbitrarily to exclude using the person's past experiences in showing him how he is misunderstanding and being maladaptive in his contemporary life.

There are a variety of forms of group psychotherapy. In some of these—for example, psychodrama, or *Gestalt* therapy—the individual, or a small group of individuals, re-experiences or explores intense feelings in the presence of the group. The group may later comment, but even before they do, their presence makes the feelings of the participants more vivid. In group psychotherapy, *per se,* all members of the group and the leader as well are in constant interaction. The topics may be consultative (problems experienced by the members), autobiographical (the background of the patients), goal-solving (plans for the future), as well as the educational effects of discussing how the various members feel about one another. Another variety of group therapy is family therapy, in which all members of the family, forming a natural group, discuss their problems of living in the presence of a psychotherapist.

Since the emphasis in this chapter is on finding a psychotherapist rather than recommending a given style of treatment, I will refer you at the end of the book to several volumes where you may find authoritative descriptions of the various modalities of group psychotherapy. In my own practice I prefer to work with my patients simultaneously in group and individual psychotherapy.

A substantially different way of approaching psychotherapeutic problems is known as behavior therapy, or behavior modification. This is an approach to particular disabling symptoms through techniques developed in studies of the psychology of learning. It is an approach that tries to remove such emotional discomforts as phobias, sexual dysfunctioning, severe anxiety, tension, inability to be assertive, etc. There is less emphasis on the emotional relationship between the patient and therapist than in many other psychotherapies. The therapeutic goals are accomplished in a variety of ways, including the substitution of a desirable act for an undesirable one, promoting desired experiences within a context of greater relaxation, and so forth. This technique is described by Joseph Wolpe.

A technique that was out of favor for many years but is regarded now as a promising approach to emotional problems is hypnosis. It is useful for symptom removal, relaxation, recovery of lost memories, insight, and so forth.

The next question to be asked is "Who does psychotherapy?" Psychotherapy is conducted by individuals who use a wide variety of titles, such as psychotherapist, psychoanalyst, psychiatrist, psychologist, psychiatric social worker, marriage counselor, group therapist, counselor, psychiatric nurse, etc.

There is a wide variety of theoretical and technical approaches to psychotherapy and some technical problems concerning the difference or boundary line between psychotherapy and counseling. My own attitude is a simple one: Regardless of professional title or theoretical basis, your consultant had better be experienced, well trained, mature, and humane. It is likely that with increasing amounts of experience, the actual procedures used by different practitioners evolve toward some common techniques and approaches, at least insofar as the same type of person is being treated.

If you believe that obtaining a competent psychotherapist has some similarity to proceeding through a semi-uncharted jungle, your perception is correct. The three chief professions practicing psychotherapy are clinical psychology, psychiatry, and psychiatric social work. Typically, a clinical psychologist has the equivalent of five years of theoretical, clinical, and practical training beyond a bachelor's degree and receives the Doctor of Philosophy degree. His formal training in mental and emotional phenomena is longest. The psychiatrist is always a physician who subsequently specializes in emotional disorders. He may get further training in special institutes (as may members of other professions), or by working for several years in hospitals or outpatient clinics. The psychiatric social worker generally receives the Master of Social Work degree for two years of training after a bachelor's degree. Some social workers now take further training toward a doctoral degree in their area. In addition, there are specialized training institutes which take individuals who may or may not have any of the three degrees mentioned (Ph.D., M.D., M.S.W.) and train their candidates in various forms of psychotherapy. There are also specialized university programs which offer certificates or degrees in addition to those mentioned—e.g., in Human Relations, School Psychology, Family Counseling, etc.

An additional form of training is the personal psychotherapy of the psychotherapist. If you know that the person you are planning to consult with is the graduate of a recognized institute, it is more than likely that he or she has had several hundred hours of personal psychotherapy. This willingness to cope with the maladjustments and emotional discomforts in his own life for personal reasons, as well as the resultant increased understanding and ability to help his patients, is a quality that you should seek. It is legitimate for you to inquire whether your psychotherapist has had personal analysis. If he says no, or is evasive or defensive, then this would be a factor in your decision.

Are there particular ways of determining the competence of the therapist? There are many ways, and it is difficult to make an accurate judgment merely from the presence of credentials. However, if the potential consultant has few or no formal credentials, then you should be particularly wary. You may be dealing with a self-appointed do-gooder who is cheerfully accepting a fee for tinkering with your mind. Again, there are large numbers of highly unqualified, unethical charlatans in the area of psychotherapy. An idealistic, optimistic brochure is no substitute for intelligence and training.

After you have determined what degrees the individual has, you might inquire whether the therapist is licensed or certified. In every state a physician (psychiatrist) must be licensed. In many states psychologists are licensed or certified by the appropriate department in the state that controls professional practice. In the remainder, there are additional means for determining whether the practitioner is highly regarded by his fellow professionals. Some state psychological associations have certification procedures in the absence of formal licensure. For psychologists and psychiatrists, there are examining boards to identify practitioners of above-average competence. In psychology, you might ask if the consultant has received a diploma in clinical psychology from the American Board of Professional Psychology. In the case of psychiatrists, the comparable board is in Neurology and Psychiatry. Some social workers are certified by the National Council of Social Workers.

To summarize so far, you should be able to find out your potential therapist's degree and from which university it was obtained, whether he is licensed, whether he has had personal psychotherapy, is a graduate of a specialized institute, and how many years he has been in practice.

Where should you seek therapy? For example, can you get adequate service at a clinic? This question can be answered only in terms of the fee you can pay. The moderate range of fees for private practice in the New York City area is from $15 to $25 for individual psychotherapy and from $10 to $15 for a one-and-one-half to two-hour group-therapy session. It is more likely that you would get satisfactory service if you sought help from a private practitioner. The reason is simple. The therapists at clinics range from the most talented down to beginners learning under supervision. I have myself functioned at clinics, both as a beginner and, after many years of experience, in the role of both supervisor and clinician. Some of my trainees did estimable work with their patients. However, in those cases where there is not a suitable match between your characteristics and the *assigned* therapist, then there may be considerable inflexibility on the part of the administration in making a change. Of course, if you have heard that a talented therapist is at a clinic, you might ask to be assigned to him or her. On the other hand, the rate of turnover in personnel is quite large. You stand a fair chance of having your therapist leave the clinic to enter private practice or because he has completed his training program. Private practitioners occasionally give up or transfer their practices, but the rate is much lower than for therapists engaged in clinics.

There are several ways of locating a psychotherapist. Referral by a satisfied patient is one. The local psychological or psychiatric or social work society is another. Yellow-page (telephone) listings are possible but problematic, since, unless there are state laws, anybody can offer his services. Furthermore, in some localities, should you desire a psychiatrist, all medical practitioners are listed together so that you could not identify which of them is in the practice of psychiatry.

I would like to make a comment about the practice of psychotherapy by psychiatrists. There are many conditions in which a knowledge of medicine is necessary for the diagnosis and treatment of emotionally related conditions. Some examples are the various psychosomatic conditions, such as colitis, some forms of asthma, etc. However, the knowledge of medicine as such is not necessary for the practice of psychotherapy in the large majority of cases. Nevertheless, it does place a burden of common sense on the non-medical practitioner to know the characteristics of emotional problems which conceal medical conditions and if in doubt to make a referral to a competent physician or specialist. Furthermore, the training of psychiatrists for private practice is considerably variable. Some of the finest psychoanalytic institutes in the world are open only to physicians (this is unjust and harmful to the general public, but it is a fact, anyway). On the other hand, intensive training in the treatment of a hospitalized population is not sufficient training for the type of emotional discomforts experienced by the large majority of people. Therefore, it is as necessary to ask about the training of your potential psychiatrist as about any other practitioner you may consult.

What are some of the personal characteristics that the prospective patient might seek in a psychotherapist? This is based on my personal experience as a patient, practitioner, trainer of therapists, and supervisor, and the formal studies of a number of psychologists (Parker, 1969, 1972c, 1972d). Let me state first of all that therapy should be a healing experience. I assume that therapy is a complex interpersonal experience, involving both emotional and intellectual qualities.

PERSONAL QUALITIES:

1. *Broad personal experience.* The therapist ought to be empathic to a variety of life styles and able to relate to patients who express themselves in terms of literature, music, and other modes of entertainment and communication. He must be aware of current events, scientific developments, and social conditions that affect the well-being and career of his patients. He ought to be able to relate or make referrals when problems arise in such areas as law and medicine.

2. *Self-awareness.* Through his own therapeutic experience in individual and preferably group therapy as well, he ought to know his own needs, sensitivities, motives, frustrations, deprivations, vulnerabilities, etc. It is vital that he be able to understand his own anger and what he does to stir up anger in others so that he can then cope with the projections of his patients.

3. *Accepting attitude.* The therapist ought to be relatively free of prejudices, permissive of others to express their doubts and anger to him, and generally non-punitive. He ought not to be grandiose about his capacities, because then he will make frustrat-

ing demands for change. As you know from our chapters on "Your Defective Brain" and "Your Childish Values," people are slow to change. They probably do so more rapidly in a kindly than in an authoritarian atmosphere.

4. *Emotionally expressive.* The therapist ought to express warmth, caring, liking, interest, respect, support, and compassion. He ought to be also able to show anger, fear, and resentment in useful ways—i.e., point out to his patient what is unreasonable and provocative about him.

5. *Personal security.* A secure therapist maintains his identity apart from his need for the support of his group or individual patients. This permits the patient to develop his own identity and independence.

PROFESSIONAL QUALITIES:

6. *Leadership.* If he is a group leader he must strike a balance between accepting responsibility and a kind of aggressive stimulation which has been found to cause a high proportion of "casualties" in group participants (Yalom and Lieberman, in *Progress in Group and Family Therapy,* edited by Clifford Sager and Helen Kaplan).

7. *Appropriate intellectual qualities.* The therapist must have a firm grasp of the professional knowledge in psychotherapy and also training in making adequate interventions. His training should be in a wide variety of areas, including the biological background of behavior. He should be alert to new trends in behavioral science to avoid becoming not only out of date but also cultistic.

8. *Ethical and dependable.* The patient has a right to expect that his therapist be non-exploitative emotionally and economically, that he be trustworthy in a crisis, consistent, and capable of maintaining confidentiality.

In connection with ethical responsibilities, there is an increasing number of reports of psychotherapists having sexual relationships with their patients. For example, the article "The Sensuous Psychiatrists" by Dr. Phyllis Chesler in June 19, 1972, *New York* magazine gives some specific experiences of women who have had sexual experiences with their psychotherapists. It is clearly an example of mutually self-destructive behavior when this occurs. While it is theoretically possible for a sexually competent and humane therapist to have a beneficial effect on a patient with a sexual problem, the therapist is not in an unbiased position to judge. Most of the reported experiences were emotionally damaging. Since sexual feelings do occur between therapists and patients (on both sides), and it is normal, what should you do if these occur? It seems to me that they should be openly discussed and that very likely they represent some frustrations the patient is revealing. It is to Sigmund Freud's credit that he recognized the "transferential" nature of these experiences from one situation to another. He would state bluntly to his patients that they were coming to see him for help and not for love! Thus, if the pressure toward overt sexuality comes from the therapist, emotional common sense indicates that you terminate the relationship abruptly.

Patients' attitudes toward their therapists were studied by Strupp, Fox, and Lessler in *Patients View Their Psychotherapy*, (1969). It was found that "psychotherapy was seen by our respondents as an intensely personal experience. More important, the therapist's warmth, his respect and interest, and his perceived competence and activity emerged as important ingredients in the amount of change reported by the patient. The more uncertain the patient felt about the therapist's attitude toward him the less change he tended to experience."

Today, the majority of people seem distressed by the original psychoanalytic model in which an authoritative, somewhat distant therapist "reflects" his impression of what the patient is doing, while adding as little as possible of his own personality. As someone stated, he wouldn't want a therapist that "lets you do all the talking. You have to do all the work." People seek psychotherapeutic assistance from somebody who is positive, who perceives his client as an individual, somebody with warmth and breadth of experience.

It has been a long road down the bypaths of self-destructive behavior. I hope that through recognizing in yourself some of the landmarks, you have been able to use this book as a guide toward fulfillment and emotional common sense and away from self-destructiveness.

Bibliography

Abraham, K., "The Influence of Oral Eroticism on Character Formation." *Selected Papers*. New York: Basic Books, 1953.

Adler, A., *The Science of Life*. New York: Anchor Books, 1969.

———, *What Life Should Mean to You*. New York: Grosset & Dunlap, 1931.

Brady, J.V., "Psychophysiology of Emotional Behavior," in Bachrach, A.J. (ed.), *Experimental Foundations of Clinical Psychology*. New York: Basic Books, 1962.

Breuer, J., and Freud, S., *Studies in Hysteria*. New York: Basic Books, 1957.

Bruner, J.S., *Toward a Theory of Instruction*. Cambridge, Mass.: The Belknap Press of Harvard University Press, 1966.

Bry, A., *Inside Psychotherapy*. New York: Basic Books, 1972.

Cattell, R.B., *The Scientific Analysis of Personality*. Chicago: Aldine, 1965.

Chesler, P., "The Sensuous Psychiatrists," *New York* magazine, June 19, 1972.

Clark, R.A., *Einstein: The Life and Times*. New York: World Publishing Company, 1971.

Cuber, J.F., "Sex in Five Types of Marriage," in *Sexual Behavior*, January 1972.

D'Andrade, R., "Sex Differences and Cultural Institutions," in Maccoby (ed.), *The Development of Sex Differences*. Stanford; Stanford University Press, 1966.

Darwin, C., *The Voyage of the Beagle*. New York: Anchor Books, 1962.

Dollard, J., and Miller, N.E., *Personality and Psychotherapy*. New York: McGraw-Hill, 1950.

Ellis, A., and Abarbanel, A (eds.), *The Encyclopedia of Sexual Behavior*. New York: Hawthorn Books, 1967.

Freud, A., *The Ego and the Mechanisms of Defense*. New York: International Universities Press, 1953.

Goldenson, R.M., *The Encyclopedia of Human Behavior*. Garden City, N.Y.: Doubleday, 1970.

Gordon, J.E. (ed.), *Handbook of Clinical and Experimental Hypnosis.* New York: The Macmillan Company, 1967.

Guilford, J.P., *Personality.* New York: McGraw-Hill, 1950.

Hamburg, D., and Lunde, D., "Sex Hormones in the Development of Sex Differences in Human Behavior," in Maccoby (ed.), *The Development of Sex Differences.* Stanford: Stanford University Press, 1966.

Harlow, R., "Motivation as a Factor in the Acquisition of New Responses," Nebraska Symposium on Motivation. Lincoln, Nebraska: University of Nebraska Press, 1953.

Healy, W., "The Most Complex Material in All Nature," in Beck, S.J., and Molish, H.B., *A Reader in Clinical Psychology.* Glencoe, Illinois: The Free Press, 1959.

Hurley, J., "Cultural Process and Evolution," in Roe, A., and Simpson, G.G. (eds.), *Behavior and Evolution.* New Haven: Yale University Press, 1958.

Kaplan, H.L., and Sadock, B. (eds.), *Comprehensive Group Psychotherapy.* Baltimore: Williams and Wilkins, 1971.

Kinsey, A.C., Pomeroy, W.B., and Martin, C.E., *Sexual Behavior in the Human Male.* Philadelphia: Saunders, 1948.

Kinsey, A.C., and Gebhard, P.H., *Sexual Behavior in the Human Female.* New York: Pocket Books, 1965.

Knapp, P.H., "Image, Symbol and Person," in *Archives of General Psychiatry,* 1969.

Lamb, H., *Charlemagne.* New York: Bantam Books, 1954.

Lamb, W., and Turner, D., *Management Behavior.* New York: International Universities Press, 1969.

Laughlin, H. *The Neuroses.* Washington: Buttersworth, 1967.

Leopold, L.C., and Ardrey, R., "Toxic Substances in Plants and the Food Habits of Early Man," in *Science,* 1972.

Lorenz, K., *On Aggression.* New York: Harcourt, Brace & World, 1963.

Maccoby, E.E., "Sex Differences in Intellectual Functioning," in Maccoby (ed.), *The Development of Sex Differences.* Stanford: Stanford University Press, 1966.

Mark, V.H., and Ervin, F.R., *Violence and the Brain.* New York: Harper & Row, 1970.

Maslow, A.H., "Deficiency Motivation and Growth Motivation," in Mahrer, A., and Pearson, L. (eds.), *Creative Developments in Psychotherapy.* Cleveland: The Press of Case Western Reserve University, 1971.

Masters, W.H., and Johnson, V.S., *Human Sexual Response.* Boston: Little, Brown, 1966.

Parker, R.S., "The Varieties of Resistance in Group Therapy Considered from the Point of View of Adaptation." *The Psychiatric Quarterly,* 1967, 41, 525–535.

———, "Poetry, a Therapeutic Art in the Resolution of Psychotherapeutic Resistance." In J. Leedy (ed.), *Poetry Therapy.* Philadelphia: Lippincott, 1969.

———, "Anger, Identification, and Irrational Target Selection." In R.S. Parker, (ed.), *The Emotional Stress of War, Violence, and Peace.* Pittsburgh: Stanwix House, 1972a.

———, "The Patient Who Cannot Express Pain." In R. S. Parker (ed.), *The Emotional Stress of War, Violence, and Peace*. Pittsburgh: Stanwix House, 1972b.

———, "Can Group Therapy Be Harmful to the Individual?" *J. Clinical Issues in Psychology*. 1972c, 3, 22–24.

———, "Some Qualities Enhancing Group Therapist Effectiveness." *J. Clinical Issues in Psychology*. 1972d, 4, 26–28.

Peter, L.J., and Hull, R., *The Peter Principle*. New York: Bantam Books, 1969.

Piaget, J., and Inhelder, Barbel, in *Psychology Today*, 1970, Vol. 3.

Piotrowski, Z.A., *Perceptanalysis*. Philadelphia: Ex Libris, 1965.

Portnoy, I., "The Anxiety States," in Arieti, S. (ed.), *American Handbook of Psychiatry*, Vol. 1. New York: Basic Books, 1959.

Reik, T., "Forgiveness and Vengeance" (1928), in *The Compulsion to Confess*. New York: John Wiley & Sons, 1959.

Robbins, L.H., "Archaeology in the Turkana District, Kenya," in *Science*, 1972.

Romer, A.S., "Phylogeny and Behavior with Special Reference to Vertebrate Evolution," in Roe, A., and Simpson, G.G. (eds.), *Behavior and Evolution*. New Haven: Yale University Press, 1958.

Sager, C., and Kaplan, H. S. (eds.), *Progress in Group Therapy*. New York: Brunner/Mazel, 1972.

Stekel, W., *Sadism and Masochism* (1929). New York: Liveright, 1953, 2 vols.

Strupp, H., Fox, R.E. and Lessler, K., *Patients View Their Psychotherapy*. Baltimore: Johns Hopkins Press, 1969.

Thomas, A., Chess, S., and Birch, H.G., *Temperament and Behavior Disorder in Children*. New York: New York University Press, 1969.

———, *A Treasury of the World's Best-Loved Poems*. New York: Crown Publishers, 1961.

Wechsler, D., *The Measurement and Appraisal of Adult Intelligence*. Baltimore: Williams and Wilkins, 1958.

Wendorf, F., Said, R., and Schild, R., "Egyptian Prehistory: Some New Concepts," in *Science*, 1970.

Wolpe, J., *The Practice of Behavior Therapy*. Elmsford, N.Y.: Permagon Press, 1969.

Wood, A.E., "Interrelations of Humans, Dogs, and Rodents," in *Science*, 1972.

Yalom, I. D. *The Theory and Practice of Group Psychotherapy*. New York: Basic Books, 1970.

Zung, W., "The Pharmacology of Disordered Sleep," in Hartman, E. (ed.), *Sleep and Dreaming*. Boston: Little, Brown & Co., 1970, pp. 123–146.

Index

73 74 75 76 77 9 8 7 6 5 4 3 2